AF269456

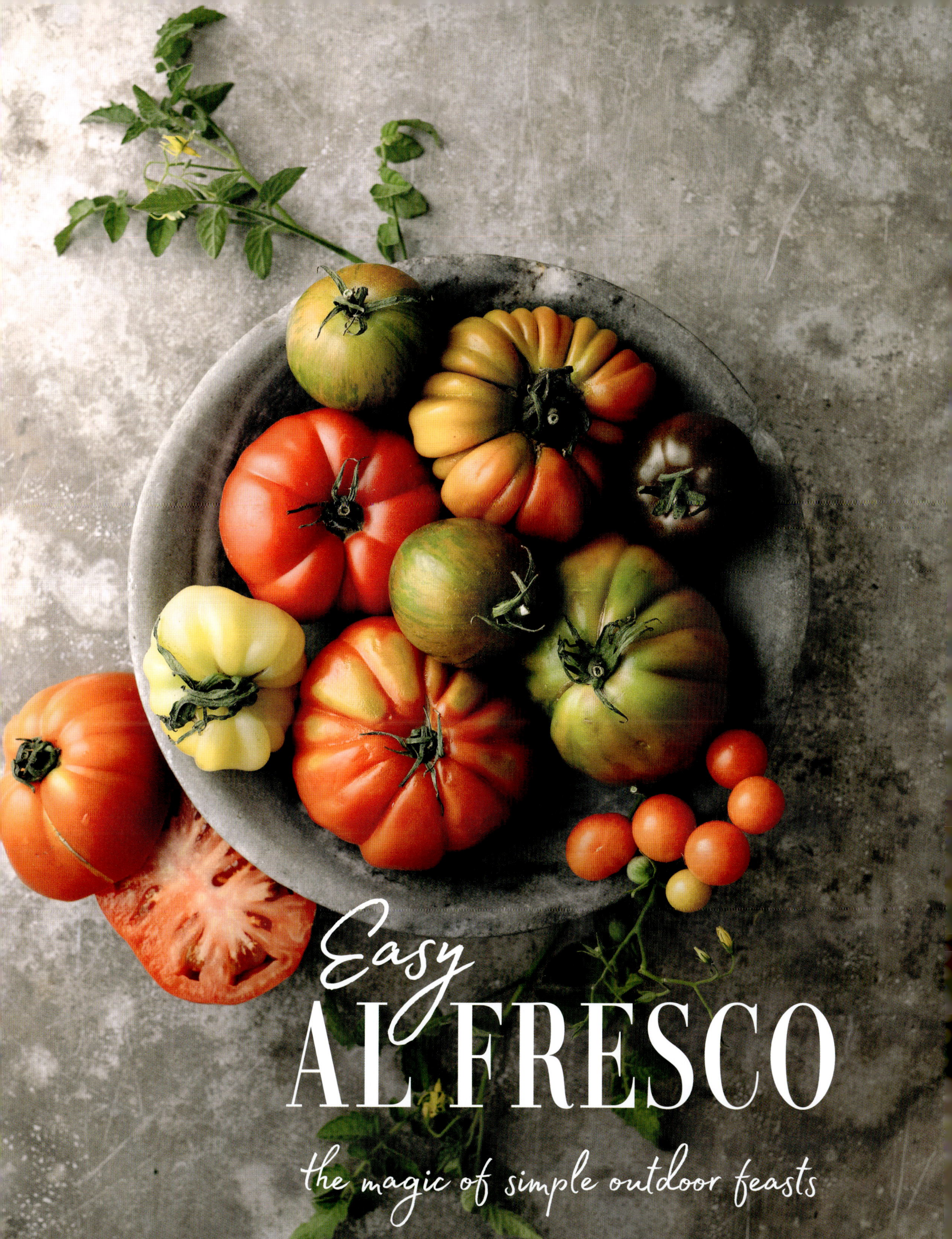

Easy
AL FRESCO
the magic of simple outdoor feasts

Easy
AL FRESCO
the magic of simple outdoor feasts
Ilse van der Merwe
Photography by Tasha Seccombe

Contents

Introduction

Something magical happens when we mindfully enjoy food in the open air. Everyday eating is elevated to a multi-sensory, recreational activity – a heady combination of fresh air and flavours, of outdoor sounds and views of nature – usually accompanied by good conversation, spontaneous laughter and true relaxation. Food has always been a catalyst in bringing people together, hopefully for a good time with friends and loved ones, but the al fresco event becomes so much more than the sum of its parts. We come away energised, nurtured (in more ways than one) and deeply satisfied.

This book celebrates that magic. Simple, scrumptious food, enjoyed and often also cooked in the open air without the need for fancy equipment, so that you can be truly present in those precious times and the new memories you're making.

As South Africans, we share an inherent, spirited love for outdoor cooking and entertaining, whether it is to light a fire and braai, or simply gather and share food under starry African skies. Yet, in an era of frequent scheduled power outages in South Africa (load-shedding), many of us have resorted to mediocre and usually unhealthy take-away meals to counter the cooking challenges that come with a lack of electricity. But when you really start to look, there are so many recipes that you can prepare without the use of electricity. A simple, one-plate gas hob is a great, inexpensive and lightweight investment, while its accompanying small gas canister can be replaced from most supermarket shelves. If you're not a fan of gas, a basic outdoor fire will do the trick. And to reassure you, there are many recipes in this book that are prepared without any heat source at all, so you have dozens of options. From dips and snacks to salads, mezze, sandwiches, seafood, meat and many vegetarian alternatives – I've got you covered. My motto is to keep it as fuss free and effortless as possible, so that you and I can enjoy these moments to the fullest.

The phrase 'al fresco', which borrows the Italian words for 'in the fresh/cool air', is a globally accepted term across many languages for eating outdoors – although not applied within this context in Italy, interestingly. 'Al fresco' also has a universal accompanied association of being informal, simple, fresh, relaxing and leisurely. To take it even further, 'destination dining' has become a modern phrase referring to the influence that your surroundings have on your dining experience. Simply put, a humble plate of freshly grilled fish enjoyed on a seaside verandah at sunset tastes different to the same plate of fish eaten in a stuffy dining room a block away.

Open your windows wide, leave the sliding door ajar, set a table outside and feel your soul come alive. Whether you're at home in the middle of suburbia on your porch, at a caravan park next to the ocean, a lapa in the bushveld, or perhaps a stoep in the Karoo, this book is your recipe guide to creating magical moments in the open air. Even if you do have access to plenty of electricity and stoves and fancy equipment, you may still want to keep it 'off grid' – just because you can!

TOOLS

Your access to kitchen tools and electricity will vary depending on where you are. At home, you may have access to anything you can think of, but at your favourite self-catering cabin there are probably fewer utensils and perhaps no machines. When camping in the middle of nowhere, you'll be cooking with an even more basic set-up – which makes it all the more magical when you can create scrumptious meals using just a handful of basic tools and ingredients. This book caters for the most rudimentary of kitchen set-ups, mostly without electricity. None of the recipes require an oven or electrical food processing tools, just a small working surface and sometimes a heat source. However, I've included notes for when you do have access to a full kitchen.

You'll see a list of 'tools' at the beginning of each recipe – the items you'll need to prepare the dish in the picture. Have everything ready before you start, including the ingredients. Note: I haven't mentioned regular cutlery or crockery for eating, as well as table linen, décor, glassware, etc. I'm sure you're creative enough to sort that on your own, according to what's available to you.

COOKING WITH FIRE

The purpose of this book is not to teach you how to braai or how to interpret a fire – I trust that you have the knowledge to do it, or that you'll have a companion who can help if you don't know how, or that you'll take the leap of figuring it out on your own like millions of others before you. This is also not essentially a braai book, even though many of the recipes can or should be cooked over a fire. When I indicate a fire or hot coals or a kettle braai, I won't mention that you'll also need wood/briquettes, firelighters and a lighter, so please take those into consideration.

'REPLACING' AN OVEN

The controlled 'heat box' environment that an oven provides can only partially be matched by a kettle braai (e.g. Weber, Big Green Egg), especially when it comes to baking. That's one of the reasons why I haven't included many baking recipes in this book, because not everyone owns a kettle braai. If you do have one, it's a good idea to read up on how to create indirect heat easily with the briquettes – a set-up that closely matches oven conditions for a limited period.

KEEPING THINGS COLD

Many raw ingredients require refrigeration, so that's something you can't do without. Fridges will keep food cold between scheduled power outages, but a simple cooler box with a few ice packs will also suffice for a day trip to the middle of nowhere.

MAKING THE MOST OF STORE-BOUGHT 'SHORTCUTS'

I've intentionally included the use of ready-made, store-bought products, such as tikka marinade, Thai curry paste, barbecue spice, marinated sun-dried tomatoes, falafel premix, rotisserie chicken, etc. It will cut hours from your prep time when your goal is to keep it effortless, especially when you don't have access to electricity or power-driven food processing tools. The recipes in this book vary from simple to ultra-simple – in many instances they're more of a serving suggestion than an actual recipe – allowing you to prepare food without stress or effort, using minimal tools and accessible ingredients.

SEASONS

Al fresco cooking is by no means limited to summertime. You can do it all year long with the right gear and perhaps a canopy for those rainy days. Dreary weather has never been a deterrent for South Africans wanting to enjoy their food outdoors!

A NOTE ON FISH AND SEAFOOD SUSTAINABILITY

Choosing sustainably sourced seafood is extremely important to me. Not many of us are lucky enough to be able to buy fresh seafood from a seaside fish shop where you can ask about the origin of the catches. However, the frozen sections of many supermarkets provide a wonderful selection these days, so be sure to look out for the blue MSC label on frozen seafood packaging (only awarded to wild fish or seafood from fisheries that have been certified to a scientific measure of sustainable fishing). Also take a look at sustainable online seafood suppliers, such as greenfish.co.za and fishwithastory.co.za (Abalobi app) or blueoceanmussels.co.za – they all supply the highest quality sustainably sourced local seafood. For more information on the subject, see also the South African Sustainable Seafood Initiative (WWF SASSI) website (wwfsassi.co.za).

DESSERTS

So many homemade desserts rely on electric mixers, ovens, freezers or longer refrigeration. For this reason I want you to view the short dessert chapter as 'serving ideas' that may be reimagined with many other ingredient substitutes. If you're already making an entire meal from scratch, my advice is to keep it simple and serve a sweet ending that is either store-bought (such as ice lollies or a tub of ice cream, or a pretty plate of chocolate treats) or something that you can easily put together, like a fresh fruit salad, a self-help Eton mess station or a scrumptious warm sauce with store-bought ice cream. Keep it fresh and seasonal where fruit is concerned and add a few extras such as chopped nuts or crumbled fudge as an ice cream topping. I promise you, everyone will be happy, and you'll be free to enjoy the last stage of the feast without a fuss.

WASTE MANAGEMENT

Cooking through 80 recipes in a relatively short time frame for the sake of creating the styled photographs that you see in this book is a tremendous privilege, but also comes with great responsibility in terms of food consumption and waste management. I've always been acutely aware of food's primary nutritional role, even though my work and recipes focus so intensely on the secondary psychological role of food in terms of togetherness, caring for each other, self-care and cooking as an act of love. During the production of this book, most of the food that you see on these pages was distributed to the production team and the people who clean in and around my home. I have an efficient system of buying inexpensive, stackable, reusable containers that I label repeatedly with masking tape and a marker; this way I can easily donate food or keep track of what's in my fridge. Anything that's not fit for human consumption by the end of the day is composted in a dedicated area next to our home – our neighbour is a farmer who makes sure that everything eventually ends up as nutrition for the earth. I also have a strict recycling system at home for food packaging. We can all make a difference, no matter how insignificant it may seem.

Breads

Quick-griddled yoghurt flatbreads

This recipe has changed the way I think about baking and serving bread; it can be prepared in a flash from scratch, so you can do it at the last minute if necessary. The flatbreads are beautifully soft, and because they're yeast free, there's no need for lengthy kneading or proofing at all. They're a total game changer.

MAKES 4 FLATBREADS

TOOLS: MIXING BOWL | SPOON | WORKING SURFACE OR WOODEN BOARD | ROLLING PIN (SEE NOTE) | HEAT SOURCE | GRIDDLE PAN OR REGULAR PAN

250 g (1¾ cups) white bread wheat flour, plus extra for dusting
15 ml (1 Tbsp) baking powder
5 ml (1 tsp) salt
250 g (1 cup) double cream plain yoghurt

To a large mixing bowl, add the flour, baking powder and salt, then stir well. Add the yoghurt and stir until lumps form, then mix by hand, kneading lightly until it comes together in a ball. On a lightly floured surface, divide the dough into four equal portions. Pat each one out (dusting with a little extra flour) until 5–8 mm thick, in oval or round shapes (or roll out with a rolling pin).

Preheat a griddle pan over medium-high heat, then cook the flatbreads on both sides until puffed up and lightly charred (2–3 minutes a side, depending on the heat of the pan and the thickness of the dough). Remove from the pan and serve at once or at room temperature, as part of a mezze spread for dipping, or as a side with your choice of main course and salad.

Note

· *Although the flatbreads are easy to pat into disc shapes on a floured surface/board, if you have access to a rolling pin, you can use it to roll them out instead.*

Braaibroodjie flatbread

I devised this recipe for Roodeberg Wines in 2022, based on the Quick-griddled yoghurt flatbreads (page 13), but with the added toppings of a braaibroodjie. The result was so delightful that I've since made it more than a couple of times in my home oven, and it's a solid hit with friends and family. If you have access to an oven, it's easiest to bake it that way, but if you are without electricity but have access to a kettle braai, you will achieve a similar result with slightly smokier flavours. It's a crowd-pleasing bread and a beautiful, generous addition to the centre of a table.

MAKES 1 LARGE FLATBREAD

TOOLS: MEDIUM TO LARGE MIXING BOWL | SPOON | ROLLING PIN (OPTIONAL) | LARGE WOODEN BOARD | KNIFE | GRATER | KETTLE BRAAI (OR REGULAR OVEN)

250 g (1¾ cups) white bread wheat flour, plus extra for dusting

15 ml (1 Tbsp) baking powder

5 ml (1 tsp) salt

250 g (1 cup) double cream plain yoghurt

30 ml (2 Tbsp) melted butter

±80 ml (⅓ cup) chutney

150—200 g (1½—2 cups) grated mature cheddar

1—2 large (or a handful small) tomatoes, thinly sliced

½ red (or white/brown) onion, thinly sliced into rounds

salt and pepper, to taste

a handful fresh wild rocket leaves, for garnishing (optional)

For the flatbread dough, place the flour, baking powder and salt in a mixing bowl and stir well. Add the yoghurt, then use a spatula or wooden spoon to mix until it becomes clumpy. Continue mixing by hand until most of the flour is incorporated and then shape into a ball. Dust a clean working surface generously with flour, then pat out the dough with floured hands into a large oval (or use a rolling pin to roll into a rectangular-ish shape), about 35 × 25 cm.

FOR KETTLE BRAAI COOKING: Prepare a kettle braai for indirect heat with coals on the sides, leaving the middle open for a large oval flatbread.

Place the topping ingredients next to the kettle braai, then transfer the flattened dough to the centre of the kettle braai and close the lid. After 6–8 minutes carefully turn the bread over, brush with the melted butter and spread the chutney evenly over the surface with the back of a spoon. Now top with the grated cheese, tomatoes, onion and a little salt and pepper. Close the lid again for another 8–12 minutes or until the bread is golden brown all over.

Remove from the braai and transfer to a wooden serving board, top with some rocket leaves, then slice into portions. Serve hot or at room temperature.

FOR OVEN COOKING: Preheat the oven to 220°C. Bake the flattened dough on a lightly floured baking tray for 8 minutes. Remove from the oven, then brush with the melted butter, add the toppings and bake for another 12 minutes or until golden brown. Serve as indicated above.

Soft flour tortillas

If you're away for the weekend and far from the shops, chances are you might have a handful of very basic pantry ingredients on hand to make these easy, soft, flour tortillas. Once cooked, fill them with a dollop of mayo (or labneh or sour cream), your choice of shredded meat (optional, perhaps leftovers from last night's braai) and some sliced tomatoes and red onions, and you have a simple yet scrumptious lunch.

MAKES 12 TORTILLAS

TOOLS: LARGE MIXING BOWL | TEASPOON | MIXING SPOON | TEA TOWEL | CLEAN WORKING SURFACE OR LARGE CUTTING BOARD | ROLLING PIN (OR SOMETHING SIMILAR SUCH AS A CLEAN WINE BOTTLE) | LARGE SKILLET OR PAN | HEAT SOURCE | SPATULA FOR TURNING

455 g (3¼ cups) stone ground white bread wheat flour
7.5 ml (1½ tsp) salt
5 ml (1 tsp) baking powder
80 ml (⅓ cup) extra virgin olive oil (or neutral vegetable oil, but I prefer EVOO)
250 ml (1 cup) lukewarm water

Place the flour, salt and baking powder in a large bowl and mix well (by hand or using a spoon). Add the oil and water and mix to a sticky dough, then continue to mix and knead to a smooth ball – it only takes a few minutes. Divide the dough into 12 equal pieces, cover with a damp tea towel and leave to rest for at least 30 minutes. Roll each piece out on a floured surface to a circle of about 20 cm in diameter, then toast it in a medium-hot skillet or pan on both sides until lightly charred and fully cooked (about 2 minutes a side). Remove from the heat, stack as you go, and cover with a clean tea towel to keep the tortillas soft while you work.

Best served at once (warm), with your choice of fillings such as shredded slow-cooked meat, tomato salsa, beans, sour cream, guacamole, fresh coriander, lettuce, red onion.

Note

- *These tortillas freeze very well.*

Easy beer bread

I can't claim to have discovered the alchemy of this easy recipe as it's been around for a long, long time. It's probably the easiest no-knead bread out there, made with self-raising wheat flour, beer and some salt. Stir together, scrape into an oiled pan and bake (oven, pot over fire or kettle braai). Crunchy exterior, fluffy inside, perfect for a simple campfire 'kuier', served with lashings of butter and jam. If you like, be creative with your own additions of grated cheese, herbs or spices.

MAKES 1 LOAF

TOOLS: MIXING BOWL | SPOON | ROUND OR RECTANGULAR SMALL TO MEDIUM FLAT-BOTTOMED CAST-IRON POT (WITH LID) AND HOT COALS, OR SMALL TO REGULAR BREAD TIN AND OVEN | CLEAN KITCHEN CLOTH | BREAD KNIFE | CUTTING BOARD

500 g self-raising wheat flour (or 3½ cups white bread wheat flour with 3½ tsp baking powder)
340 ml beer (regular lager or almost any craft beer)
7.5 ml (1½ tsp) salt
a little cooking oil or olive oil, for the pan or pot

Add the flour, beer and salt to a mixing bowl, then stir to create a sticky, well-mixed dough.

FOR FIRE COOKING: Thoroughly oil the inside of a rectangular cast-iron bread pot with lid or a flat-bottomed cast-iron pot with a lid. Scrape the dough into the pot and smooth the surface as much as possible. Cover with the lid and bake over medium-hot coals (also placing some hot coals on top of the lid) for 50–60 minutes or until golden brown and fully cooked.

FOR OVEN BAKING: Preheat the oven to 180°C. Thoroughly oil the inside of a bread tin, then scrape the dough into the tin and smooth the surface as much as possible. Bake for 1 hour, then turn out the loaf and wrap it in a clean kitchen cloth for about 15 minutes, to soften the crust. Serve warm or at room temperature, spread with butter.

Polenta and sweetcorn bread

This recipe is based on an American-style corn bread with a South African sweetcorn loaf twist. It's delicious dunked into saucy stews and potjies, and heavenly when served warm with very ripe brie and a drizzle of honey. It's an any time of the day treat.

SERVES 6 (AS A SIDE)

TOOLS: MEDIUM–LARGE MIXING BOWL | SPOON | WIDE MEDIUM TO LARGE FLAT-BOTTOMED CAST-IRON POT (ROUND OR RECTANGULAR, WITH LID) AND HOT COALS OR LARGE BREAD OR CAKE TIN AND OVEN | KNIFE

170 g (1 cup) polenta
140 g (1 cup) white bread wheat flour
10 ml (2 tsp) baking powder
5 ml (1 tsp) salt
1 × 410 g can cream-style sweetcorn
250 ml (1 cup) buttermilk (see below)
2 extra-large eggs
vegetable or olive oil, for oiling pot or tin
30—45 ml (2—3 Tbsp) butter

Place the polenta, flour, baking powder and salt in a mixing bowl and stir well. Add the sweetcorn, buttermilk and eggs, then stir until the batter mixture just comes together but with no floury lumps (don't mix too long).

FOR FIRE BAKING: Thoroughly oil the inside of a cast-iron pot, then transfer the dough into the pot and smooth the surface as much as possible. Cover with a lid, then bake over medium-hot coals (also placing some hot coals on top of the lid) for 20–25 minutes or until golden brown and fully cooked. Remove from the fire and spread the butter over the top of the bread, giving it a few minutes to melt before serving.

FOR OVEN COOKING: Thoroughly oil the inside of a bread or cake tin, then transfer the dough into the tin and smooth the surface as much as possible. Bake in a preheated oven at 200°C for 20–25 minutes or until golden brown and fully cooked. Remove from the oven and spread with the butter over the top of the bread, giving it 10–15 minutes to soak in before serving.

Slice and serve straight from the pan.

If you don't have access to buttermilk, mix 2 teaspoons of white vinegar with 1 cup of milk and leave for 5 minutes to thicken before using.

Seeded crusty pot bread

This beautiful, textural, crusty loaf is baked in a preheated cast-iron pot with lid – the high heat gives the exterior the look of a proper artisanal loaf, yet this simple recipe is a quick stir-together method with no kneading, only some folding. Great texture makes amazing sandwiches. It's my favourite new low-effort bread recipe of the year!

SERVES 6/MAKES 1 POT BREAD

TOOLS: LARGE MIXING BOWL | TEASPOON AND CUP MEASURES | WOODEN SPOON OR SILICONE SPATULA | DAMP TEA TOWEL | SHEET OF NON-STICK BAKING PAPER | SHARP KNIFE | DEEP CAST-IRON POT WITH LID (ABOUT 25 CM DIAMETER) | COOLING RACK

280 g (2 cups) white bread wheat flour
280 g (2 cups) brown bread wheat flour
80 g (½ cup) linseeds
70 g (½ cup) sunflower seeds
7 g (2 tsp) instant yeast
10 ml (2 tsp) salt
475 ml (just less than 2 cups) warm water

Place the flours, seeds, yeast and salt in a large mixing bowl and stir to mix. Add the water and stir well to form a sticky dough (make sure to work out all the floury bits). Cover with a damp tea towel and leave to proof at room temperature for 1 hour until doubled in size. After the first 30 minutes of proofing, prepare the heat source as stated below, preheating the empty pot and lid at high heat. After the full hour of proofing, use a wooden spoon or silicone spatula to fold the dough from the outer bottom to the middle, 12 times, turning the bowl after each fold – 'right around the clock.' Transfer the folded dough to a lightly floured surface, dust the top with more flour, and shape into a neat ball with a smooth top (tuck the sides in towards the bottom centre). Place the dough on a sheet of baking paper, transfer to a round bowl roughly the same size as the pot (or use the cleaned mixing bowl), and leave to rest for 15 minutes, covered with a damp tea towel. Transfer the rested dough to the preheated pot (lift it by using the overhanging baking paper), make two slits in the top of the dough using a sharp knife, cover with the heated lid and bake as stated below.

FOR KETTLE BRAAI COOKING: Bake in a preheated kettle braai over indirect heat for 30 minutes (kettle lid closed, vents open), then remove the lid of the pot and bake for another 15 minutes (kettle lid closed, vents open). Remove from the kettle braai and leave to cool on a wire rack.

FOR FIRE COOKING: Place the covered pot on a stable grid or potjie stand over medium-hot coals, placing a layer of coals on the lid. Cook for about 40 minutes until golden brown and fully cooked, turning the pot slightly every 15 minutes for even heat distribution. Remove from the fire and leave to cool on a wire rack.

FOR OVEN COOKING: With the oven preheated to 230°C, bake in the centre of the oven for 30 minutes (in the preheated pot), then remove the lid and bake for another 10–15 minutes, uncovered. Remove from the oven and leave to cool on a wire rack.

Cheese-stuffed pull-apart bread

This is a clever and simple trick to take a store-bought loaf to the next level. It's a crowd pleaser every time. Use your favourite cheese and change up the herbs to whatever you have on hand.

MAKES 1 LARGE LOAF

TOOLS: LONG-BLADED SERRATED BREAD KNIFE | FOIL OR BAKING PAPER | GRATER | CUTTING BOARD | CHOPPING KNIFE | SMALL SAUCEPAN

1 large fresh or day-old sourdough loaf (or wood-fired ciabatta)
200 g (2 cups) roughly grated mature cheddar (or your choice of cheese)
a handful finely chopped fresh Italian parsley or thyme (optional)
salt and pepper, to taste
125 g (½ cup) butter, melted

Using a very sharp bread knife, slice the bread diagonally in two directions to create diamond shapes, but do not cut all the way through to the bottom (i.e. leave the loaf intact). Place the loaf on a large sheet of foil. (If you will be using an oven, you could use baking paper instead of foil.) Stuff the cheese into all the cuts, along with the parsley or thyme (if using) and season all over with salt and pepper. Pour the melted butter all over the sliced cracks, letting it seep into the stuffing. Wrap the foil over the top to enclose the loaf, then set aside until ready to cook.

FOR KETTLE BRAAI COOKING: Place the foil-wrapped loaf over indirect heat in the kettle braai, close the lid and cook for about 15 minutes until golden at the edges and the cheese is fully melted. Remove from the heat and transfer to a wooden board, carefully peeling the foil to the sides.

FOR FIRE COOKING: Place the foil-wrapped loaf on a grid over medium-hot coals for 15–20 minutes, turning every few minutes, until golden at the edges and the cheese is fully melted. Remove from the heat and transfer to a wooden board, carefully peeling the foil to the sides.

FOR OVEN COOKING: Place the foil-wrapped loaf on a baking tray in a preheated oven at 200°C and bake for 15 minutes, then open up the foil and continue to bake for another 10–15 minutes until golden at the edges and the cheese is fully melted. Remove from the oven and transfer to a wooden board, carefully peeling the foil to the sides.

Serve warm at a shared table, with guests pulling off portions of hot, cheesy bread.

Dips
& spreads

Tahini yoghurt dip

For me, this is the Middle East in a bowl. It is so wonderfully versatile – with salads, crudités, pita bread, falafels, lamb, chicken or even fish. It's super easy to assemble, and it lasts well in the fridge.

MAKES 375 ML (1½ CUPS)

TOOLS: MEDIUM MIXING BOWL | SPOON | CUP MEASURE | TABLESPOON | PAN AND HEAT SOURCE (FOR TOASTING SESAME SEEDS) | SERVING BOWL

250 ml (1 cup) double cream plain yoghurt
60 ml (¼ cup) tahini
15 ml (1 Tbsp) fresh lemon juice
5 ml (1 tsp) ground cumin
2.5 ml (½ tsp) smoked paprika, plus extra for dusting
salt and pepper, to taste
15 ml (1 Tbsp) extra virgin olive oil, for drizzling (optional)
toasted sesame seeds, for sprinkling (optional)

Combine the yoghurt, tahini, lemon juice, cumin and paprika in a mixing bowl and stir. Season with salt and pepper, taste to see if you need to adjust any of the seasoning, then transfer to a serving bowl. Drizzle with a little olive oil and sprinkle over toasted sesame seeds (if using) and a dusting of smoked paprika. Serve with your choice of bread, crackers or vegetables, or even meat to dip into or to spoon over.

For a more pourable consistency (turning it into a dressing), add 2–3 tablespoons of water.

Chunky tartare

When you're serving the Grilled seafood platter (page 149) or almost anything fried in oil (page 73 for Beer-battered veggie strips), a zippy tartare sauce is a crowd-pleasing favourite for dipping. These days I lighten tartare with some plain yoghurt instead of mayonnaise only; it makes a huge difference, especially because I love scooping large amounts of this saucy dip at a time. Instead of chopping gherkins by hand, use a box grater – it works like magic.

MAKES ± 375 ML (1½ CUPS)

TOOLS: SMALL MIXING BOWL | MEASURING CUP | TEASPOON | CHOPPING BOARD | GRATER | CHOPPING KNIFE | MIXING SPOON

125 ml (½ cup) mayonnaise
125 ml (½ cup) double cream plain yoghurt
10 ml (2 tsp) Dijon mustard
10 ml (2 tsp) fresh lemon juice
125–250 ml (½–1 cup) sweet and tangy pickled gherkins, roughly grated
15 ml (1 Tbsp) roughly chopped capers
a small handful fresh dill and/or parsley, finely chopped
Lemon rind, finely grated (optional)

Stir all the ingredients together in a small mixing bowl. If using, sprinkle with lemon zest. Cover and refrigerate until ready to serve. Serve with your favourite seafood or fried food, or as a sandwich spread with cheese and lettuce. It will keep in the fridge for up to one week.

Cheat's truffle aïoli

Aïoli is a traditional Mediterranean-style garlic and olive oil emulsion – or in layman's terms, a garlic-flavoured mayonnaise. With added truffle flavour, it's one of the most delicious and luxurious condiments you can imagine. If you're looking for a low-tech way of creating this delightful dip/spread, and you'd rather skip the make-from-scratch part of the mayonnaise, just stir together a few simple ingredients with a few drops of truffle oil (a little goes a very long way).

MAKES 250 ML (1 CUP)

TOOLS: MEDIUM MIXING BOWL | SPOON | FINE GRATER | CUP MEASURE | TABLESPOON

250 ml (1 cup) good quality mayonnaise
1 (or more) clove/s garlic, finely grated or crushed
15 ml (1 Tbsp) fresh lemon juice
a few drops truffle oil
a pinch salt

Combine all the ingredients in a mixing bowl. Transfer to a serving jug and serve immediately, or keep refrigerated and use within a few days.

Notes

- Truffle-flavoured oil is sold in small quantities; it might seem excessive or expensive, but it will last long as you use only a few drops at a time. It is marvellous on softly scrambled eggs with some grated parmesan.

- If you're one of the lucky ones to have access to fresh Perigord truffles during the very short winter season window, use a tiny quantity of freshly grated truffle instead of the oil for a truly authentic, earthy truffle flavour.

Serve alongside freshly grilled fish and potatoes, spread on steak sandwiches, or use as a dip for crudités.

Dill and cucumber labneh

This is a tasty spin on a more traditional minty tzatziki. I love the luxurious texture and luscious thickness of labneh – a fresh, spreadable cheese made from strained yoghurt. With the addition of grated cucumber and chopped dill, it becomes a fresh-tasting spread that makes the most delicious sandwich filling, mezze dip or crostini topping with cold smoked trout.

MAKES ±500 ML (2 CUPS)

TOOLS: KNIFE | MIXING SPOON | MIXING BOWL | GRATER

½ English cucumber
a small bunch fresh dill, finely chopped
250 ml (1 cup) plain labneh
15–30 ml (1–2 Tbsp) fresh lemon juice
salt and pepper, to taste
15 ml (1 Tbsp) extra virgin olive oil

Slice the cucumber in half lengthways, then grate it from the inside towards the skin, discarding the last bit of skin. Add the grated cucumber to a mixing bowl, along with the chopped dill, labneh, lemon juice and some salt and pepper. Mix well, then transfer to a serving bowl and drizzle with a little olive oil. Cover and refrigerate until ready to serve.

Serve as part of a mezze spread with fresh bread, or as directed above.

Notes

- *Because the labneh is so thick, you don't have to scoop out the watery seeds of the cucumber, unless you really want to – I usually use the whole cucumber.*

- *Make your own labneh from natural, stirred (unthickened) yoghurt by straining it through a clean muslin cloth overnight.*

Retro cottage cheese dip

This is the 'doopsous' that we grew up with in the 1980s and '90s. My mother must have made it hundreds of times; it's só old-school but such a crowd pleaser. I've tried to substitute the tomato sauce with 'classier' options such as artisanal chutney, but the original recipe remains my favourite. Back in the day, my mom also added condensed milk, but it's honestly sweet enough as is, so I don't add that anymore. This dip is completely smashable with a packet of your favourite potato/corn crisps (crinkle cut, cheese curls, triangular corn chips, etc.) and can sometimes even be a guilty-pleasure dinner for one.

MAKES ± 250 ML (1 CUP)

TOOLS: MEDIUM MIXING BOWL | SPOON | GRATER OR KNIFE

1 × 250 g (1 tub) plain smooth cottage cheese (low fat or full cream)
45–60 ml (3–4 Tbsp) mayonnaise
30–45 ml (2–3 Tbsp) tomato sauce (preferably All Gold)
10 ml (2 tsp) Dijon mustard
5–10 ml (1–2 tsp) Worcestershire sauce
15—30 ml (1–2 Tbsp) grated or very finely chopped white/brown onion

Combine all the ingredients in a mixing bowl until thoroughly mixed. Serve cold or at room temperature in a dip bowl alongside your favourite potato crisps.

Yoghurt guacamole

I love traditional all-avocado guacamole, but this version with added yoghurt just lightens it up into a lovely pale green, anytime dip. Because avos turn brown easily after being released from their skins, this dip is best served straight after preparation, but it will last for a few hours in the fridge, covered. It is fabulous served with crispy tortilla chips, or as a saucy topping for burgers, sandwiches and tacos (from page 110).

MAKES ±375 ML (1½ CUPS) (DEPENDING ON THE SIZE OF THE AVOS)

TOOLS: KNIFE | SPOON | FORK | MIXING BOWL

1 large or 2 smaller ripe avocado/s
125 ml (½ cup) double cream plain yoghurt
15–30 ml (1–2 Tbsp) fresh lemon juice
2.5 ml (½ tsp) ground cumin (optional)
salt and pepper, to taste

Scoop the avo flesh into a mixing bowl, then mash it as finely as possible with a fork. Add the yoghurt, lemon juice and cumin (if using), then season generously with salt and pepper. Mix well, taste, and adjust the seasoning if necessary. Serve immediately, or cover and refrigerate for up to 2 hours before serving.

I find the best way to remove the skin of an avo is to halve it, remove the stone and scoop out the flesh in one go with a dessertspoon.

Sweet and spicy tomato and red pepper salsa

My sister regularly serves this crunchy, sweet, spicy salsa as an appetiser with tortilla chips. The chunky texture is a welcome alternative (or addition) to most other creamy dips. The secret ingredient is a sweet and spicy Peppadew piquanté pepper chutney – an excellent store-bought product that can also be used as is on boerewors rolls or braaibroodjies instead of regular stone fruit chutney. The success of this salsa is in the fine texture of the chopped bits, so be a little patient and see how finely you can chop them! It's well worth the effort.

MAKES 500 ML (2 CUPS), SERVES 6

TOOLS: CHOPPING BOARD | CHOPPING KNIFE | MIXING BOWL | SPOON

2 large ripe tomatoes, finely chopped
1 red pepper, pith and seeds removed, and finely chopped
1 small red onion, finely chopped
a small bunch fresh coriander leaves, finely chopped
80 ml (⅓ cup) sweet and spicy Peppadew piquanté pepper chutney
a squeeze fresh lemon juice, to taste
salt and pepper, to taste

Combine all the ingredients in a mixing bowl and mix well. Cover and refrigerate until ready to serve. Garnish as desired, then serve with tortilla chips (perhaps also with the Yoghurt guacamole, page 39), as a filling for tacos, or as an accompaniment to grilled fish.

Chunky rocket and walnut pesto

Making pesto without a food processor might seem like a daunting task, but a chunky, hand-chopped pesto can be a delightful alternative to the more traditional smooth version, and it's not too laborious at all. Rocket leaves are punchy in flavour and easily available, while walnuts have a tender crunch that make them easy to hand chop.
If you don't have parmesan, use any full-flavoured, semi-hard, mature cheese that you have on hand.

Serve this pesto as part of a mezze spread for dipping crusty bread, or over freshly grilled steak, stir through cooked baby potatoes or roasted vegetables for a flavourful warm salad, or serve with freshly cooked pasta. It's also delicious as a sandwich spread (page 113 for Party-size caprese sandwich) with sliced cheese, tomato, ham or salami and crunchy lettuce.

MAKES 250 ML (1 CUP)

TOOLS: CHOPPING BOARD | CHOPPING KNIFE | MEDIUM MIXING BOWL | GRATER | TABLESPOON | QUARTER-CUP MEASURE

a bunch fresh rocket leaves, rinsed, well drained and finely chopped
a handful walnuts, finely chopped
±60 ml (¼ cup) finely grated parmesan
salt and pepper, to taste
±15 ml (1 Tbsp) fresh lemon juice (or to taste)
±60 ml (¼ cup) extra virgin olive oil (or to taste)

Combine all the ingredients in a mixing bowl until well mixed. Taste and adjust seasoning if needed. Add more olive oil or lemon juice for a runnier consistency. Serve cold or at room temperature in a dip bowl as part of an antipasti or mezze spread (or see more serving suggestions above).

Notes

- If you have a food processor, just pulse all the ingredients together for a few seconds, scraping the sides.

- During the late winter season and early spring, use any young caper leaves you may have in your garden to make a really wonderful caper pesto; the leaves are totally edible and have a delicious, peppery taste. Rinse the leaves before use.

Biltong pâté

I originally created this recipe for Anthonij Rupert Wines in 2022. It was such a hit in our home that we've since made it quite a few times. The key to the beautiful spreadable consistency is to use fine biltong powder. It's so easy to prepare, just stir and serve.

MAKES ±375 ML (1½ CUPS)

TOOLS: MEDIUM MIXING BOWL | CHOPPING BOARD | CHOPPING KNIFE | SPOON | FINE GRATER

100 g (±¾ cup) fine biltong powder
250 ml (1 cup) sour cream
60 ml (¼ cup) mayonnaise
5 ml (1 tsp) wholegrain or Dijon mustard
5 ml (1 tsp) finely grated lemon rind
5–10 ml (1–2 tsp) fresh lemon juice
a handful fresh chives and/or Italian parsley, finely chopped
salt and pepper, to taste

Stir all the ingredients together in a mixing bowl until thoroughly combined. Taste, then adjust the seasoning if needed, mixing well. Serve as a spread for crackers or crostinis or toasted bread.

Canned tuna pâté

Sometimes you need to be creative with a can of fish, whether you're camping in the middle of nowhere or unexpected guests arrive at home. Canned tuna is such a versatile product, but you can also use canned salmon, canned middlecut or canned smoked sardines.

MAKES ±250 ML (1 CUP)

TOOLS: CAN OPENER | CHOPPING BOARD | CHOPPING KNIFE | MEDIUM MIXING BOWL | SPOON

1 × 170 g can tuna (shredded or chunks) in brine, well drained
125 ml (½ cup) sour cream
2–3 spring onions, finely chopped
a handful fresh chives, finely chopped
2.5 ml (½ tsp) smoked paprika (optional)
a squeeze fresh lemon juice
salt and pepper, to taste

In a mixing bowl, stir all the ingredients together. Taste and adjust the seasoning if necessary. Refrigerate until ready to serve. Serve with fresh or toasted bread, or spoon onto toasted crostinis for a festive starter, topped with extra chives.

Notes

· *I personally prefer canned fish in brine, but you can also use fish in oil; just be sure to drain off as much of the brine/ oil as possible (press the loosened lid of the can down on the solids).*

· *This pâté also makes a delicious sandwich filling; just add shredded lettuce and perhaps some sliced tomato.*

Leftover braaied or smoked fish pâté

If you're lucky enough to have braaied a large fresh fish (see Grilled yellowtail with spiced apricot glaze on page 137) for your previous meal, there might be some leftovers to turn into this fabulous festive pâté. Beige-coloured pâté can sometimes look a little bland, so I've topped it with a bright green layer of chopped herbs.

MAKES ±500 ML (2 CUPS)

TOOLS: MEDIUM MIXING BOWL | FORK | CHOPPING KNIFE | CHOPPING BOARD

2–3 cups flaked and deboned cooked fish
60 ml (¼ cup) good quality mayonnaise
230 g (1 cup) plain cream cheese
30 ml (2 Tbsp) fresh lemon juice
a handful fresh herbs (e.g. parsley, chives, dill), finely chopped, plus extra for sprinkling
salt and pepper, to taste

Using a fork, mix all the ingredients together in a mixing bowl until well combined. Taste and adjust the seasoning if needed, or add more lemon juice if you prefer. Serve 'as is' in a small bowl, or transfer to a shallow bowl where you can smooth the top and sprinkle generously with finely chopped herbs. Cover and refrigerate until ready to serve. Serve with fresh or toasted bread, or on crackers.

Appetisers
& mezze

Linefish ceviche
with avocado and grapefruit

I created this recipe for Spier Wines in 2022 - so very fresh and delicious. The secret to great ceviche lies in sourcing the freshest fish. Talk to your fishmonger about your ceviche plans and make sure they offer you only the freshest catch. Great quality, sustainably caught, flash-frozen fish fillets will also do – I've used fresh sea bass from Wild Peacock in Stellenbosch as well as frozen kingklip from Greenfish (online shop) for this recipe and both worked incredibly well.

SERVES 4 AS A STARTER OR MEZZE

TOOLS: CUTTING BOARD | LONG-BLADED SHARP KNIFE | CHOPPING KNIFE | DEEP BOWL WITH LID (OR REUSABLE COVER) | SERVING PLATTER

300–400 g very fresh line fish fillets, pin-boned (e.g. sea bass, kingklip or other firm white fish)
juice of 2 limes
juice of 1 lemon
salt, to taste
1 large ripe avocado, cubed
1–2 ripe grapefruit (or blood orange), thinly segmented
± ½ cup finely diced cucumber
¼ red onion, very finely sliced
a handful fresh coriander, roughly chopped
salt and pepper, to taste
a few baby radishes, finely sliced (optional)
1–2 Tbsp (15–30 ml) extra virgin olive oil

Using a sharp long-bladed knife, slice the fish into thin slivers, then transfer them to a deep bowl. Pour the lime and lemon juice all over (make sure it reaches all the pieces), season lightly with salt, cover and leave to cure in the fridge for 15–20 minutes or until the flesh has just turned opaque (white). Pour off any excess juice and transfer the slices of ceviche to a serving platter. Top with avocado, grapefruit, cucumber, red onion, chopped coriander and a sprinkle of salt and pepper. Scatter over the radishes (if using), and drizzle with olive oil. Serve immediately.

Note

- Ceviche can be made a few hours ahead; just prep to the stage where you pour off excess citrus, then cover and refrigerate. When ready to serve, arrange on a plate and top with the remaining ingredients.

Balsamic tomatoes *and figs on crostini*

Invest in an aged balsamic vinegar and the freshest extra virgin olive oil for this simple recipe – there's just no substitute for the deep flavour. The combination of ripe tomatoes and black figs works exceptionally well when in season, but you could also just use one or the other. Served on freshly toasted crostini, it makes an elegant starter that will please a crowd.

SERVES 4–6 AS A SNACK OR STARTER

TOOLS: CUTTING BOARD | CHOPPING KNIFE | MEDIUM MIXING BOWL | MIXING SPOON | BREAD KNIFE | PAN AND HEAT SOURCE (OR GRID AND HOT COALS)

2–3 large ripe tomatoes, diced or quartered
4–6 ripe black figs, sliced into smaller chunks
15 ml (1 Tbsp) extra virgin olive oil, plus extra for the crostini
30 ml (2 Tbsp) aged balsamic vinegar
a handful fresh basil leaves, roughly chopped or whole
salt and pepper, to taste
1 baguette loaf, sliced

Place the tomatoes and figs in a bowl, along with the olive oil, balsamic vinegar and basil. Season with salt and pepper and give it a gentle stir, then set aside to marinate while you make the crostini. Place the sliced baguette on a plate or working surface, then brush the facing sides with oil. Toast on the oiled side briefly in a medium-hot pan until golden (or toast on a grid over medium-hot coals), then arrange on a platter or plate. Top each crostini, toasted-side up, with a spoonful of the balsamic mixture and serve immediately.

White anchovies *with artichokes, capers, lemon and herbs*

This dish may not even count as a 'recipe', because it's a combination of some of my favourite store-bought antipasti on a plate with a few fresh ingredients to round it off. Heavenly, super simple, fuss free, crowd pleasing. I've finally come to believe that this isn't cheating, it's clever entertaining.

SERVES 4–6 AS PART OF A MEZZE SPREAD

TOOLS: SERVING PLATE | CHOPPING BOARD | CHOPPING KNIFE

150 g marinated white anchovy fillets
280 g marinated artichoke hearts in oil (not brine)
30 ml (2 Tbsp) baby capers
a squeeze fresh lemon juice
a handful fresh herbs, finely sliced (e.g. parsley, dill, chives, basil)
salt flakes and freshly ground black pepper
crostini or fresh bread, for serving (optional)

Drain the anchovy fillets and arrange them on a serving plate (reserve the liquid, see Notes). Drain the artichokes and arrange them on top of the anchovies (reserve the liquid, see Notes). Top with the capers, lemon juice and a scattering of herbs. Season with salt and pepper.

Notes

- *Marinated white anchovy fillets differ from darker preserved anchovies in oil. Look for them in the seafood mezze section of some supermarkets.*

- *Use the reserved marinated liquid or oil in your next salad dressing, or as a drizzle for freshly grilled steak or freshly baked potatoes - it's extremely flavourful.*

Smashed burrata

If you're not familiar with burrata, it's a cousin of fior di latte and also a fresh-style mozzarella, usually made from cow's milk (or sometimes from buffalo milk), with a runny, creamy centre. It's phenomenal topped with pesto, but you can also simply serve it with extra virgin olive oil, a few capers, salt and pepper.

SERVES 2–4 AS A SNACK OR STARTER

TOOLS: SERVING PLATE OR PLATTER | FORK

2 × 125 g balls burrata
extra virgin olive oil, for drizzling
a few teaspoons baby capers
a few spoons Chunky rocket and walnut pesto (page 43) (optional)
salt flakes and freshly ground black pepper

Place the burrata balls on a serving plate and use a fork to roughly smash them to reveal the runny centres. Drizzle generously with olive oil, then top with some capers, pesto (if using), salt flakes and freshly ground pepper. Serve with fresh or toasted bread, scooping the cheese onto the slices and dipping the bread into the creamy oil that gathers in the plate.

Scoop onto the freshest warm bread you can find, or give your artisanal loaf a quick toast before tucking in. The Balsamic tomatoes and/or figs (page 54) also make a wonderful combination, if you want to turn it into a simple feast.

Retro brandied shrimp cocktail lettuce cups

Ah, who can resist the fabulously retro Marie Rose seafood cocktail sauce? I recently started making it again, and the reaction from my guests is always so positive – big smiles, tales to relate from the 1980s, empty plates. I add a generous splash of brandy to my sauce, which gives it a little more depth of flavour and a playful, festive edge. The sauce isn't only good on shrimp or prawns, but on almost any seafood and even chicken or pork. The cocktail mixture makes a great sandwich filling too.

SERVES 4–6 AS A SNACK

TOOLS: SMALL MIXING BOWL | SPOON | MEDIUM POT WITH LID | MEDIUM MIXING BOWL | CHOPPING BOARD | CHOPPING KNIFE | SERVING PLATE

125 ml (½ cup) good quality mayonnaise
30 ml (2 Tbsp) tomato sauce (preferably All Gold)
5 ml (1 tsp) Worcestershire sauce
5 ml (1 tsp) fresh lemon juice
15 ml (1 Tbsp) brandy
2.5 ml (½ tsp) smoked paprika, plus extra for serving
salt and pepper, to taste
250 g shrimp meat, thawed if frozen, peeled and deveigned
water, for cooking
1–2 celery stalks, finely chopped
a small bunch fresh chives, finely chopped
2 heads baby gem lettuce, leaves separated and rinsed

To prepare the Marie Rose sauce, add the mayo, tomato sauce, Worcestershire sauce, lemon juice, brandy and smoked paprika to a small mixing bowl. Season with salt and pepper, mix well and set aside.

For the shrimp, add a little water (about 1 cm deep) to a pot and bring to a simmer with a pinch of salt. Add the shrimp, cover with a lid and cook for about 2 minutes until just cooked and opaque. Remove from the heat and drain the water, running the shrimp under cool water to stop the cooking process. Transfer to a clean tea towel to drain any excess water (blot from the top too), then leave to cool for a few minutes. To a medium mixing bowl, add the cooked drained shrimp, the prepared sauce, chopped celery and half the chives, then mix well. Refrigerate until ready to serve.

To serve, arrange the lettuce leaves on a serving plate, then scoop 1–2 tablespoons of the cocktail mixture into each lettuce 'cup'. Top with chopped chives and a light sprinkle of smoked paprika. Serve immediately.

Pan-fried feta *with honey and thyme*

I absolutely love warm, grilled feta, and usually prepare it in my oven on a lined baking tray, drizzled with olive oil and herbs – very easy. But it's just as easily done in a pan over any heat source. Feta doesn't melt completely like most other cheese, but it does tend to stick to a frying pan. Yet, with a light coating of egg and store-bought crumbs, you can achieve a crispy outer layer and a warm, soft inner. I've included instructions for pan-frying (with a light crumb coating) as well as oven grilling (without a crumb coating); the choice is yours. Serve it warm with toasted bread, perhaps also with some Balsamic tomatoes and/or figs (page 54) on the side.

SERVES 6 AS A SNACK OR MEZZE

TOOLS: BOWL FOR EGG | BOWL FOR CRUMBS | LARGE FRYING PAN (PREFERABLY NON-STICK) WITH HEAT SOURCE | SPATULA | SERVING PLATE

200 g firm feta (rounds or square slabs)
1 egg, lightly whisked
80 ml (⅓ cup) store-bought breadcrumbs
30–45 ml (2–3 Tbsp) extra virgin olive oil
a few sprigs fresh thyme, woody stalks discarded, plus extra for serving
15–30 ml (1–2 Tbsp) honey, for drizzling
freshly ground black pepper, to taste

FOR PAN COOKING: Have the feta, whisked egg and breadcrumbs (each in separate bowls) ready next to your frying station. Heat the oil in the pan over medium heat. When the oil is hot, dip each slab of feta into the egg and then into the crumbs until well coated, then place in the hot pan. Fry on both sides until golden brown (about 2 minutes a side). Sprinkle lightly with some of the thyme leaves, then remove with a spatula and place on a serving plate. Scatter with more thyme leaves, followed by a drizzle of honey and a grinding of black pepper. Serve warm with some crostini as part of a mezze spread, or as a snack.

FOR OVEN GRILLING (WITHOUT A CRUMB COATING): Preheat the oven grill and insert an oven rack about 10 cm from the top of the grill. Place the feta rounds on a baking tray lined with non-stick baking paper, then drizzle lightly with olive oil, sprinkle with thyme leaves and a grinding of black pepper. Grill until golden brown (about 8 minutes), then remove from the oven and transfer to a serving plate. Drizzle with honey and scatter with more thyme leaves.

If you don't have breadcrumbs, try crushing some cornflakes in a plastic bag; they also work well as a crispy (gluten-free) coating.

Baby marrow, feta and mint fritters

These simple, savoury fritters are one of those anytime-of-the-day snacks. I can easily have them for breakfast topped with chunky cottage cheese and honey, but I'll also serve them as a light lunch topped with a tomato salad and rocket, or as a fireside snack served with a creamy dip (page 28 for Tahini yoghurt dip or page 31 for Chunky tartare). They also work as an elegant small canapé topped with sour cream and cold smoked trout. You can also make larger pan-sized fritters, then cut them pizza-style after cooking, for a lower effort alternative.

SERVES 4 AS A SNACK

TOOLS: CHOPPING BOARD | COARSE GRATER | FINE GRATER | MEDIUM MIXING BOWL | WOODEN SPOON | TABLESPOON | WIDE FRYING PAN WITH HEAT SOURCE | SPATULA FOR FLATTENING AND TURNING

350 g baby marrows, coarsely grated
100 g (1½ rounds) feta, crumbled
70 g (½ cup) white bread wheat flour or cake wheat flour
5 ml (1 tsp) baking powder
125 ml (½ cup) finely grated parmesan
2 extra-large eggs
a handful fresh mint, finely chopped
salt and pepper, to taste
30 ml (2 Tbsp) extra virgin olive oil

Place the grated baby marrows on a clean tea towel, then place two layers of kitchen paper on top and gently press to absorb any excess moisture. Transfer the blotted baby marrows to a mixing bowl along with the crumbled feta, flour, baking powder, parmesan, eggs and mint. Season with salt and pepper, then mix well using a wooden spoon. Heat the oil in a pan, then spoon heaped tablespoons of the mixture into the pan, leaving some space in-between and flattening them gently with a spatula. Fry on both sides until golden, puffed up and fully cooked, then remove from the pan and serve warm (see serving suggestions above).

You can also make these with a 50:50 mixture of grated baby marrow and carrot.

Smoky smashed aubergine
with garlic

Fire-roasted aubergine (also known as brinjal or eggplant) is one of the wonders of the vegetable world. So simple, yet so intensely smoky and meaty in flavour. Once you've tasted the marrowy result, topped with extra virgin olive oil, you'll wonder why you ever cooked it any other way. Scoop it onto bruschetta as a starter or as part of a bigger mezze spread.

SERVES 6 AS A STARTER

TOOLS: FORK | FIRE WITH GRID | SPOON | CHOPPING KNIFE | FINE GRATER | CHOPPING BOARD | SMALL BOWL OR CUP | SERVING PLATE

2 large or 3 medium aubergines
45–60 ml (3–4 Tbsp) extra virgin olive oil
1–2 cloves garlic, finely grated or chopped
salt flakes and freshly ground black pepper, to taste
a handful fresh Italian parsley, finely chopped
a handful roasted pine nuts, for garnishing
grated parmesan, for sprinkling

Using a fork, poke holes all over the unpeeled whole aubergines (to allow steam to escape). Arrange the aubergines on a grid over hot coals (some flames are fine) and roast for 45–60 minutes, turning often, until the outside is completely charred and wrinkly, and the inside fully cooked and very tender. Remove from the fire and transfer to a serving plate to cool slightly. Alternatively, to oven-roast the aubergines, place them on the middle rack of an oven at 230°C for 1 hour.

Meanwhile, prep the garlic oil. Place the olive oil, garlic, some salt and pepper, and the chopped parsley in a small bowl or cup and stir until mixed. Slice the aubergines in half lengthways, then use a knife or fork to roughly smash the flesh. Spoon over the oil mixture and season generously with more salt and pepper. Serve warm or at room temperature, sprinkled with pine nuts and parmasan, and toasted bread on the side.

Note

- *If you don't have fresh parsley, substitute it with a sprinkle of dried parsley or origanum.*

Grilled halloumi
with anchovy, capers, chilli and mint

If you – like me – can't resist a freshly fried slice of halloumi cheese with its crunchy exterior and almost-melted centre, the characteristic squeaky chew and all of the punchy salty astringency of chilli, anchovies and capers (hello, best pizza topping combo!), then this recipe is for you. I can eat a whole plate of it for dinner, requiring very little else other, perhaps, than a glass of chilled wooded chenin, yet this dish makes an excellent addition to any mezze spread. For those who love goat's milk cheese, a goat's milk halloumi is the ultimate prize.

SERVES 4 AS A SNACK

TOOLS: CHOPPING KNIFE | LARGE NON-STICK PAN | SPATULA | SERVING PLATE | CHOPPING BOARD | SPOON

30 ml (2 Tbsp) extra virgin olive oil
±300 g good quality halloumi cheese, sliced into 4–5 mm-thick slices
2–3 anchovy fillets in oil, drained and chopped
15 ml (1 Tbsp) baby capers
2.5 ml (½ tsp) dried chilli flakes
a few fresh mint leaves, finely sliced or shredded
salt and pepper, to taste
fresh lemon wedges, for serving

In a large non-stick pan, heat the oil over medium heat, then place the halloumi slices next to one another, frying and turning them over with a spatula until golden on both sides. Transfer them to a serving plate.

In the same pan over medium heat, add the anchovies, capers and chilli flakes, stirring for a minute or two. Remove from the heat and use a spoon to sprinkle the fried contents all over the hot halloumi. Top with slivers of mint, a grinding of salt and pepper, a squeeze of lemon and some extra lemon wedges on the side. Serve warm.

Figs in blankets *with gorgonzola*

'Pigs in blankets' is a classic British term for pork sausages wrapped in bacon, grilled to toasty perfection. Slices of fruit wrapped in prosciutto is probably the fresher Mediterranean version, but it improves even further when that slice of smoky charcuterie is toasted over a fire, revealing the luscious juices of the warmed fruit and an oozing centre of gorgonzola.

SERVES 3–4 AS A SNACK

TOOLS: KNIFE | AT LEAST 12 TOOTHPICKS | GRID AND HOT COALS | BRAAI TONGS | SERVING PLATE

12 ripe black figs
100 g gorgonzola or creamy blue cheese, cut into small wedges (see Note)
12 thin slices (±150 g) prosciutto
honey, for drizzling
200 g gorgonzola, for serving (optional)
crostini or melba toast, for serving (optional)

Cut each fig at its base with a cross section, about halfway into the fig. Stuff a small wedge of gorgonzola into the cross section, then wrap each stuffed fig in a slice of prosciutto, fastening the loose ends with a toothpick. Grill over medium heat until toasty on all sides, turning often. Remove from the heat and place on a serving plate or platter. Drizzle with honey and serve with extra gorgonzola and crostini on the side (if using), and serve immediately.

Notes

- *Wedge-shaped pieces of cheese are easier to stuff into the figs than square blocks; their pointy edges should face the inside of the figs.*

- *When black figs are in season, there's no better treat than this simple recipe. Serve with a drizzle of honey.*

Beer-battered veggie strips

This is the same batter I use for beer-battered onion rings, but for these easy veggie strips I skip the milk soaking and flour dredging. Instead, I dip the veg directly into the batter and then fry them in hot oil. Economical, simple and totally delicious. The secret to making these strips really crispy, is to keep the batter cold before frying. They will eventually soften on standing, so serve them immediately after frying.

SERVES 4–6 AS A SNACK

TOOLS: CHOPPING BOARD | PEELER | CHOPPING KNIFE | BOWL FOR VEGGIES | MEDIUM MIXING BOWL | CUP MEASURE | TEASPOON | WIRE WHISK OR FORK | MEDIUM POT | TONGS | SLOTTED SPOON | KITCHEN PAPER | SERVING PLATE

2 large carrots, peeled and sliced into strips

1 small aubergine, sliced into strips

a few baby marrows, sliced into strips

140 g (1 cup) cake wheat flour

40 g (¼ cup) cornflour

5 ml (1 tsp) baking powder

5 ml (1 tsp) smoked paprika

salt and pepper, to taste

250 ml (1 cup) very cold beer

500 ml (2 cups) vegetable oil, for frying

Chunky tartare (sauce/dip), for serving (page 31)

fresh lemon wedges, for serving

Place the prepared vegetables in a bowl and refrigerate them while you make the batter.

Combine the cake wheat flour, cornflour, baking powder, paprika, salt and pepper in a mixing bowl then stir to mix. Add the cold beer and stir briefly until still slightly lumpy (do not overmix), then refrigerate. Heat the oil in a medium-size pot, uncovered, over medium-high heat to reach about 180°C (if you don't have an oil thermometer, just test a drop of batter and see if it sizzles; never heat the oil to smoking point). Drop a handful of veggie strips into the cold batter, spooning the batter to coat the strips well, then use tongs to carefully place them in the oil, one by one. Fry in batches, not overcrowding the pot, then remove with a slotted spoon and drain on kitchen paper. Transfer the strips to a serving plate and serve hot with some tartare sauce or dip (garnished as desired) on the side for dipping.

Notes

- *Always be careful when frying in hot oil, and never place the pot with oil directly over an open fire; only use a controlled heat source and ensure that children aren't anywhere near it.*

- *Only use very cold beer — it's the key to a crispy result that stays crispy.*

- *Serve the strips straight after cooking, at their crispiest and best.*

- *I serve a bowl of fresh vegetable strips (crudité-style) alongside the battered strips — it's nice to alternate between fresh and fried while you're snacking.*

Spiced falafel balls
with crispy curry leaves

These delightful falafel balls are made with a convenient chickpea-based premix (see Note) that is available at many supermarkets; it's a lifesaver if you don't have a food processor (or if you simply want to go the low-effort route). The addition of fried curry leaves adds an incredibly delicious nutty flavour, but is optional. Serve with a creamy yoghurt-based dip (such as the Tahini yoghurt dip on page 28) – either as a bed for the falafels or in a bowl on the side.

MAKES ±25

TOOLS: MEDIUM MIXING BOWL | SPOON | WATER JUG | WIDE HEAVY FRYING PAN WITH HEAT SOURCE | SLOTTED SPOON | KITCHEN PAPER | CHOPPING BOARD | CHOPPING KNIFE

1 × 200 g packet falafel premix
5 ml (1 tsp) smoked paprika
5 ml (1 tsp) ground cumin
5 ml (1 tsp) turmeric
200 ml (¾ cup) hot water
vegetable oil, for frying
a handful fresh curry leaves, stalks removed (optional)
250 ml (1 cup) Tahini yoghurt dip (page 28), or double plain cream yoghurt
lemon wedges, for serving

Place the premix, paprika, cumin and turmeric in a mixing bowl and stir to mix. Add the water, stir well, and continue to mix until it becomes a thick mixture that's firm enough to shape into balls. Use a spoon and wet hands to shape into small balls about 4 cm in diameter, then set aside.

Heat a generous amount of oil (at least 1 cm deep) in a deep pan or casserole, then fry the balls on all sides until golden brown. Remove them with a slotted spoon and drain on kitchen paper.

If using, immediately drop the curry leaves into the oil, turn off the heat and stir for a few seconds. When the leaves are crispy (10–15 seconds), remove them with a slotted spoon and drain on kitchen paper.

Serve the balls warm, sprinkled with salt and pepper and crispy curry leaves, on a bed of Tahini yoghurt dip (or with the dip or yoghurt on the side). Serve with a few lemon wedges on the side.

Note

- *I've had great results with Health Connection Wholefoods' Falafel Premix. It's locally made, preservative free and you basically just add water.*

Calamari piccata

The basic flavours of a classic piccata (butter, garlic, lemon, capers, parsley) work well on most seafood dishes, not only chicken and veal. I prefer squid heads and tubes for this quick-and-easy recipe, but you can use any cut of calamari you prefer. The secret to success is to start with a very hot pan and calamari that isn't wet (patting dry with kitchen paper will do the trick) to minimise the chance of a watery result.

SERVES 4 AS A LIGHT MEAL OR STARTER

TOOLS: KITCHEN PAPER (OR CLEAN CLOTH) | CHOPPING BOARD | CHOPPING KNIFE | HEAT SOURCE | LARGE CAST-IRON SKILLET (OR NON-STICK PAN) | SPATULA OR WOODEN SPOON | FINE GRATER

30 ml (2 Tbsp) extra virgin olive oil

400 g small calamari tubes and squid heads, rinsed and pat-dried with kitchen paper or cloth

30–45 ml (2–3 Tbsp) butter, plus extra

30 ml (2 Tbsp) capers

a small handful caperberries, halved

1–2 cloves garlic, finely grated

finely grated rind and juice of 1 lemon

salt and pepper, to taste

a handful fresh Italian parsley, finely chopped

lemon wedges, for serving

Heat a skillet over high heat for a few minutes until it reaches smoking point. Once hot, add the oil and the calamari (work in two batches if the pan isn't large enough), then stir to cook and char it swiftly. When the calamari starts to colour (it should only take 1–2 minutes if the pan is hot enough), add the butter and capers and caperberries, and stir for another minute. Remove the pan from the heat and stir in the garlic and lemon zest; it will continue to cook in the residual heat. Add the lemon juice and more butter – enough so you can serve the dish with some bread for dipping – and stir until the butter melts in the warm pan. Season with salt and pepper and return the pan to low heat if the butter hasn't completely melted. Add the parsley and serve at once, with some lemon wedges on the side and, optionally, crusty bread to mop up the buttery sauce.

Vegetables
& sides

The full Monty potato salad

One of my best friends, René de Wit, recently married and hosted an incredible weekend wedding celebration at Die Laaitjie, outside Robertson. For the first evening's braai festivities, her mother Anene Geustyn made the most epic potato salad I've ever had (everybody raved about it). Not only did I have a third helping, but I also finished a bowl for breakfast the next morning. After asking Anene what she had included in the salad (without quantities because she made hers to feed 25 people with LOTS of leftovers), this is my rendition of it. Thank you, Anene, for making potato salad just as fabulous as you are!

SERVES 6 AS A SIDE

TOOLS: LARGE MIXING BOWL | LARGE POT | SMALL POT | HEAT SOURCE | CHOPPING OR SLICING KNIFE | COARSE GRATER | FINE GRATER | LARGE SPOON OR SPATULA | SERVING BOWL

1.5 kg new potatoes, well rinsed (see Notes)
10 ml (2 tsp) salt
3 eggs
375 ml (1½ cups) good quality mayonnaise
250 ml (1 cup) double cream plain yoghurt
80 ml (⅓ cup) condensed milk
30–45 ml (2–3 Tbsp) lemon juice

15 ml (1 Tbsp) Dijon mustard
80 ml (⅓ cup) finely chopped onion
125 ml (½ cup) roughly grated pickled gherkins
1 clove garlic, finely grated
a handful fresh Italian parsley, finely chopped
salt and pepper, to taste

Put the potatoes in a pot and fill it with water to just cover the potatoes. Add the 10 ml of salt and place over high heat. When it comes to a boil, turn down the heat to a slow simmer. (If you like, cook the eggs at this stage in another smaller pot until hard boiled, then set them aside to cool.) Once the potatoes are just tender (test with a sharp knife), drain the water carefully. When the potatoes are cool enough to handle, but still a little warm, slice them into bite-size rounds or chunks. Peel the eggs and chop them roughly.

To a large mixing bowl add the mayonnaise, yoghurt, condensed milk, lemon juice, mustard, onion, gherkins, garlic, half the parsley and half the chopped egg. Season generously with salt and pepper, and mix well. Add the sliced potatoes on top of the sauce, then use a large spoon or spatula to fold the sauce throughout the potatoes until they are well covered. Transfer to a serving bowl, then top with the remaining parsley and boiled egg. Serve immediately, or cover and refrigerate until ready to serve. Best served at room temperature.

Notes

- *Choose baby potatoes or young oval-shaped Mediterranean potatoes with thin skins, so that you don't need to peel them. It will save a lot of prep time.*

- *A great potato salad should be generously covered in sauce, but mayonnaise alone is too rich and too thick. Adding yoghurt is the magic ingredient – don't leave it out!*

- *This salad may be made a day ahead – just keep refrigerated.*

Cranberry tabbouleh *with walnuts*

I originally created this recipe in 2022 for Perdeberg Wines' Grenache Noir, as part of a menu that also included a Middle Eastern-style spatchcock chicken. The pairing was spot on, and the wonderfully sweet, punchy, nutty spin on a traditional tabbouleh quickly became one of my go-to salads. If you haven't worked with bulgur wheat before, it's a dream for when you don't have access to electricity or a stove top, because it only needs a few minutes soaking in room-temperature water (no cooking) (see page 90 for more on bulgur wheat). It can also be prepared a day in advance, if you have access to a fridge for the night. Serve as a side with your favourite grilled meat.

SERVES 4 AS A SIDE

TOOLS: MIXING BOWL | MEASURING CUP | CHOPPING KNIFE | CHOPPING BOARD

250 ml (1 cup) fine bulgur wheat
375 ml (1½ cups) water, at room temperature
½ large cucumber, seeded and diced
½ small head broccoli, finely chopped
1 punnet fresh Italian parsley, finely chopped
1 punnet fresh mint, finely chopped (thicker stalks discarded)
½ red onion, finely diced
125 ml (½ cup) dried cranberries
100 g walnuts, lightly roasted and roughly chopped
45 ml (3 Tbsp) fresh lemon juice
45 ml (3 Tbsp) extra virgin olive oil
salt and pepper, to taste

Add the bulgur wheat and water to a mixing bowl, cover and leave to stand for 20–30 minutes until most of the water is absorbed. Drain off any excess water. Add the cucumber, broccoli, parsley, mint*, red onion, cranberries*, walnuts*, lemon juice and olive oil (*reserving some as garnish/drizzle). Season generously with salt and pepper, mix well, then cover and refrigerate until ready to serve. Garnish and drizzle with the reserved ingredients just before serving.

Strawberry salad *with goat's milk cheese, rocket and red onion*

As with the beautiful sweet-salty combo of watermelon and feta, strawberries and goat's milk cheese work wonderfully together. Strawberries are available from winter through to the end of summer, and may be used in so many surprising ways, other than a fruit salad or dessert topping. A good quality balsamic vinegar is a must, the more aged, the better. It's best to avoid the overtly sweet, syrupy nature of a 'balsamic drizzle or glaze', so look out for the real deal in terms of vinegar.

SERVES 4

TOOLS: CHOPPING BOARD | SLICING KNIFE | WIDE SALAD PLATE OR PLATTER

a medium bunch fresh rocket leaves (or watercress, or a combo of both)
250 g ripe strawberries, hulled and sliced
100–200 g plain (or with peppercorns) soft goat's milk cheese (chevin or similar), crumbled or sliced
½ small red onion, fincly sliced
freshly ground black pepper, to taste
extra virgin olive oil, for drizzling
aged balsamic vinegar, for drizzling

Arrange the rocket on a salad plate or platter, then top with the strawberries, goat's milk cheese, onions and a generous grinding of black pepper. Drizzle lightly with olive oil and balsamic vinegar. Serve immediately with extra oil and vinegar on the side.

Thai-style crunch salad
with dried mango, coconut and peanuts

I created this colourful salad for Montagu Snacks back in 2017. The texture is just heavenly – all kinds of fresh and crunchy vegetables with roasted nuts and some added sweet chewiness from the dried mango and coconut flakes. It all comes together with a zippy peanut dressing, added right before serving. This is delicious as a light lunch, but also as a side with your favourite grilled meat.

SERVES 6 AS A SIDE

TOOLS: MEDIUM MIXING BOWL | TABLESPOON | HAND WHISK | LARGE SALAD BOWL | CHOPPING BOARD | CHOPPING KNIFE | KITCHEN SCISSORS | GRATER | PEELER

FOR THE DRESSING

60 ml (¼ cup) smooth peanut butter

30 ml (2 Tbsp) fresh lime juice

30 ml (2 Tbsp) rice vinegar or apple cider vinegar or fresh lemon juice

45 ml (3 Tbsp) honey

15 ml (1 Tbsp) soy sauce

1 clove garlic, finely grated

15 ml (1 Tbsp) finely grated fresh ginger

FOR THE SALAD

1 small red cabbage, finely sliced/shredded (3–4 cups)

1 large carrot, peeled and roughly grated

250 ml (1 cup) bean sprouts

125 ml (½ cup) coconut shavings

35 g (⅓ cup) roasted salted peanuts

100 g dried mango, cut into small strips (use scissors)

a small bunch fresh coriander, roughly chopped

1–2 small red chillies, finely sliced (optional)

To make the dressing, using a hand whisk, mix all the ingredients together in a medium bowl until smooth (it might take a few minutes, but it will come together).

For the salad, place all the ingredients in a large salad bowl, but reserving some of the mango, coconut and coriander for garnishing at the end. Refrigerate at this stage until just before serving, then pour over the dressing, toss to mix, and serve with the reserved mango, coconut and coriander on top. The salad will start to wilt after coming into contact with the dressing, so don't dress it too long before serving.

Gem lettuce, avocado and blue cheese salad *with ranch dressing*

Sometimes the simplest combinations are the most successful, as with this three-ingredient salad. The secret though, is in the dressing – an American-style creamy ranch sauce that is great on anything fresh and crunchy, but just as wonderful on grilled chicken and other meat. The dressing will keep well in the fridge for up to three days, but the salad won't – prep the salad leaves and avo right before serving.

SERVES 4–6 AS A SIDE

TOOLS: SMALL MIXING BOWL WITH LID OR COVER | SPOON | MEASURING CUP (OPTIONAL) | CHOPPING BOARD | CHOPPING KNIFE | LARGE SALAD PLATTER

FOR THE RANCH DRESSING
125 ml (½ cup) good quality mayonnaise
125 ml (½ cup) sour cream
125 ml (½ cup) buttermilk
a handful fresh dill, finely chopped, plus extra for serving
salt and pepper, to taste
a squeeze fresh lemon juicc

FOR THE SALAD
2–3 heads whole baby gem lettuce, leaves separated, rinsed and drained
2 ripe avocados, depipped, peeled and sliced
100 g creamy blue cheese, crumbled

Place all the dressing ingredients in a mixing bowl, then stir to mix thoroughly. Cover and refrigerate until ready to serve.

Arrange the lettuce leaves on a salad platter, top with the avocado, pour the dressing over, then top with the crumbled blue cheese and a scattering of fresh dill. Serve immediately.

Bean and bulgur wheat salad
with dates, red onion, spinach and dill

For this recipe, I use coarse bulgur wheat – a humble grain with a pleasant chew, making it an excellent salad partner. Unlike fine bulgur wheat that only needs soaking, coarse bulgur wheat must be cooked in water for just a few minutes. I prefer to mix it with the rest of the salad ingredients (except the spinach) while warm, and include the spinach when completely cooled. This is an excellent make-ahead dish that will taste even better on the second or third day, if refrigerated. For making ahead, use shredded swiss chard – it won't wilt like baby spinach. If you can't find coarse bulgur wheat, you can also use barley – cooked for about an hour until tender.

SERVES 4 AS A SIDE

TOOLS: MEDIUM POT | FORK | LARGE MIXING OR SALAD BOWL | CHOPPING BOARD | CHOPPING KNIFE | FINE GRATER | STIRRING SPOON

250 ml (1 cup) coarse bulgur wheat
500 ml (2 cups) water
a generous pinch salt
1 × 400 g can butter beans in brine, drained
250 ml (1 cup) roughly chopped dried pitted dates
½ small red onion, finely chopped
1–2 cloves garlic, finely grated or chopped
45 ml (3 Tbsp) extra virgin olive oil
45 ml (3 Tbsp) apple cider vinegar
15 ml (1 Tbsp) wholegrain mustard
a handful fresh dill, roughly chopped
salt and pepper, to taste
30–60 g (2–3 cups) baby spinach leaves or shredded swiss chard

Place the bulgur wheat, water and salt in a pot and bring to a simmer. Cook over low heat for 12–15 minutes or until most of the water has been absorbed and the wheat is cooked and tender. Remove from the heat, fluff up with a fork, and set aside.

Meanwhile, add the beans, dates, red onion, garlic, olive oil, vinegar, mustard and dill to a salad bowl, then stir to mix thoroughly. Add the cooked warm bulgur wheat and stir it through. Taste and adjust seasoning if necessary. Just before serving, stir through the spinach leaves. Serve at room temperature.

Loaded BLT salad
with avo, croutons and crispy onions

Sometimes I love turning a classic upside-down, yet retaining the original flavours that I know and love. It's the case with this BLT sandwich-turned-salad – layers of crunchy lettuce, crispy bacon, the freshest ripe tomato, loaded with creamy avo, some pan-fried croutons (yesterday's loaf) and a jar-shaken sweet and tangy dressing.
A totally scrumptious combo.

SERVES 2 AS A MAIN, OR 4 AS A SIDE

TOOLS: TABLESPOON | LARGE WIDE FRYING PAN | SPATULA | HEAT SOURCE | CHOPPING BOARD | CHOPPING KNIFE | MEDIUM JAR WITH LID | TEASPOON | SALAD BOWL OR PLATTER

45 ml (3 Tbsp) extra virgin olive oil

2 slices bread (your choice), torn into bite-size chunks and some smaller bits

salt and pepper, to taste

250 g smoked streaky bacon

60 ml (¼ cup) extra virgin olive oil

20 ml (4 tsp) apple cider vinegar (or fresh lemon juice)

15 ml (1 Tbsp) mustard

15 ml (1 Tbsp) honey

1 small clove garlic, minced or finely grated (optional)

a medium bunch crunchy lettuce leaves (e.g. gem, romaine, iceberg)

2 large ripe tomatoes, sliced (or ±250 g small tomatoes, halved/sliced)

1 large ripe avocado, sliced

2–3 Tbsp (30–45 ml) crispy onion salad topping (optional)

Heat the 45 ml olive oil in a pan and add the bread chunks, frying them on all sides until lightly brown. Season lightly with salt and pepper. Remove the croutons from the pan, then add the bacon (in the residual oil), and fry until crisp, stirring often. Remove from the pan, set aside to cool, then chop into smaller shards.

To make the dressing, add the 60 ml oil, vinegar, mustard, honey and garlic (if using) to a jar. Season lightly with salt and pepper, close the lid and give it a vigorous shake until well emulsified. Set aside.

Arrange the lettuce, tomatoes and avocado in a salad bowl or on a platter, top generously with the croutons, bacon and crispy onion (if using), drizzle over the dressing and garnish as desired. Serve immediately.

Lentil salad

with sun-dried tomatoes, feta and herbs

Many supermarkets sell antipasti-style sun-dried tomatoes in vinaigrette – they're softer than regular sun-dried tomatoes that are preserved in oil and I find them more flavourful. Using the vinaigrette as a dressing is a short-cut to achieving wonderful results with minimum effort. The success of the lentils lies in choosing a large lentil that won't disintegrate during cooking as it needs to keep its shape.

SERVES 4–6 AS A SIDE

TOOLS: MEDIUM-LARGE POT | COLANDER | MIXING OR SALAD BOWL | CHOPPING BOARD | CHOPPING KNIFE

250 g (1¼ cups) large green/brown/black lentils (or puy or Castelluccio lentils)
240 g sun-dried tomatoes in vinaigrette, sliced into smaller chunks, liquid reserved
30–45 ml (2–3 Tbsp) extra virgin olive oil
15 ml (1 Tbsp) balsamic vinegar
salt and pepper, to taste
200 g feta, crumbled
½ small red onion, finely sliced
a bunch mixed fresh soft herbs, finely chopped (e.g. dill, parsley, chives and basil)

Place the lentils in a pot and fill with water, about 3 cm above the lentils (don't add salt yet). Bring to a simmer, then cook, uncovered, for about 20 minutes until just tender. Drain, then transfer to a mixing bowl. Add the tomatoes with their reserved liquid, the olive oil and balsamic vinegar, stirring to mix. Season with salt and pepper, then leave to cool to room temperature. Gently stir in the feta, onion and herbs. Serve at room temperature.

Notes

- As a low-effort substitute if you don't want to cook the lentils yourself, you can use 2 × 400 g cans of 'organic lentils in water' – just drain and rinse before assembling.

- For a fully vegan salad, use a vegan alternative for the feta.

- The salad may be made a day ahead, stored in the fridge and returned to room temperature before serving.

Greek-style pasta salad

This Mediterranean-flavoured pasta salad is based on a classic Greek salad with the addition of orzo – a flattish rice-shaped pasta that is also used in youvetsi, one of my favourite Greek lamb pasta dishes. But unlike a classic Greek salad that needs to be assembled right before serving, this pasta salad is slightly more forgiving and can be made up to a day in advance if kept covered in the fridge. Best served at room temperature, it's a versatile side dish for so many occasions – from picnics to a celebratory feast.

SERVES 4 AS A LIGHT MEAL OR 6 AS A SIDE

TOOLS: LARGE POT | TABLESPOON | HEAT SOURCE | WOODEN SPOON | COLANDER | CHOPPING BOARD | CHOPPING KNIFE | LARGE MIXING OR SALAD BOWL

water, for cooking

15 ml (1 Tbsp) salt

250 g orzo or rosmarino pasta

80 ml (⅓ cup) extra virgin olive oil

300 g small tomatoes, quartered or sliced

1 medium cucumber, deseeded and diced

250 ml (1 cup) pitted and halved kalamata olives

200 g feta cheese, diced

½ red onion, finely sliced

a small bunch fresh mint, finely sliced (stalks discarded), but reserve a few whole leaves for garnishing

5 ml (1 tsp) dried origanum

45 ml (3 Tbsp) red wine vinegar

salt and pepper, to taste

Fill a pot halfway with water and add 15 ml salt. Bring to a boil, add the pasta and cook for 7 minutes, stirring now and then. Drain the water and rinse for a few seconds under running water, then give it a shake and set aside to drain any excess water (stir through a tablespoon of olive oil at this point, to prevent clumping).

Place the tomatoes, cucumber, olives, feta, onion, mint and origanum in a salad bowl. Add the rest of the olive oil plus the vinegar, and stir well. Add the cooled pasta and stir through, seasoning generously with salt and pepper. Garnish, then cover and refrigerate until ready to serve, or serve at once.

Unlike with warm pasta dishes, I rinse the cooked pasta for cold pasta salads under cold running water when freshly cooked, to stop it from sticking and to cool it down faster. Drain thoroughly.

Charred broccoli and pak choy

with soy sauce, sesame and spring onion

This deeply savoury dish is incredibly simple and it all comes together in minutes, in a large frying pan. Sesame oil is the star carrier of that unmistakable nutty sesame flavour, so don't substitute it for something else. You can also top it with store-bought crispy onions for extra crunch (look for it in the refrigerated salad section), but it's optional.

SERVES 4 AS A SIDE

TOOLS: TEASPOON | TABLESPOON | LARGE WIDE FRYING PAN | SPATULA | CHOPPING BOARD | CHOPPING KNIFE | SERVING PLATE

10 ml (2 tsp) sesame oil
15 ml (1 Tbsp) vegetable oil
a small head tenderstem broccoli
4 baby pak choy, halved lengthways
30 ml (2 Tbsp) good quality soy sauce
5–10 ml (1–2 tsp) white and/or black sesame seeds (optional)
a small bunch red or green spring onions, finely sliced

Place a pan over high heat and add the sesame oil and vegetable oil. When the oil is simmering hot (but not smoking), add the broccoli and fry for about 2 minutes a side until charred, but still slightly firm. Remove the broccoli, then add the pak choy cut side-down to the same pan, charring for about 1 minute. Return the broccoli to the pan with the pak choy, then add the soy sauce and stir with a spatula to coat the vegetables on all sides while it bubbles for a few seconds. Transfer all to a serving plate and top with sesame seeds (if using) and spring onions. Serve warm.

Notes

- *If you only have a medium or small pan, work in two batches.*

- *Try this recipe with other vegetables such as chopped kale, shredded cabbage, etc.*

Spicy grilled carrots
with feta and greens

A few years ago I attended a media function at The Test Kitchen with Luke Dale Roberts, where he showcased his Big Green Egg (ceramic kettle braai) on the patio in front of the restaurant. He prepared a dish of slow-roasted carrots – the best carrots I had ever tasted. His were cooked over 4 hours on very low, controlled heat, so this recipe is a lot shorter, but aims for a similar result. Smoky, grilled vegetables are a hundred times tastier than steamed or boiled, so I urge you to try it.

SERVES 6 AS A SIDE

TOOLS: KETTLE BRAAI (OR PREPARED FIRE WITH GRID AND PERFORATED GRILL PAN) | LARGE BOWL | TABLESPOON | TEASPOON | BRAAI TONGS | SERVING PLATE

750 g small or medium carrots, washed and trimmed

45 ml (3 Tbsp) extra virgin olive oil, plus extra

5 ml (1 tsp) smoked paprika

5 ml (1 tsp) ground cumin

2.5 ml (½ tsp) dried origanum or dried mixed herbs

salt and pepper, to taste

a small bunch baby salad leaves or mixed micro herbs

100 g feta, finely crumbled

5–10 ml (1–2 tsp) sesame seeds

a squeeze fresh lemon juice

a drizzle honey

fresh rocket, for garnishing

FOR KETTLE BRAAI COOKING: Prepare a kettle braai for indirect heat. Place the carrots in a bowl, then drizzle them all over with oil and sprinkle with paprika, cumin and origanum. Season generously with salt and pepper. Using your hands, toss and rub the carrots until well coated. Wash your hands, then arrange the carrots on the grid in a row (ensuring that they won't fall through), but not directly over the hot coals. Close the lid and cook for 15–20 minutes. Open the lid and remove the carrots from the fire if they are fully cooked – they should be charred on all sides and just tender if pricked with a fork (if they need more colour, give them a quick grill directly over the hot coals). Transfer to a serving plate, top with the leaves, crumbled feta, sesame seeds, and finish with a squeeze of lemon, a drizzle of honey and a last drizzle of olive oil. Garnish with fresh rocket. Serve hot or at room temperature.

FOR FIRE COOKING: Arrange the prepped carrots on a heated perforated braai pan. Grill over medium heat for about 20 minutes, stirring now and then, until the carrots are just tender and slightly charred all over. Transfer to a serving plate and serve as above.

Note

- For oven cooking, arrange the prepared carrots on a baking sheet in a single layer, then roast in a preheated oven at 220°C for about 25 minutes until charred and fully cooked.

Grilled mealies *with harissa butter*

We all know that corn on the cob is elevated when doused with butter, and even more elevated when grilled over hot coals; this simple recipe for grilled mealies with harissa butter will really make you lick your fingers. Harissa paste is sold alongside pesto in the refrigeration aisle of supermarkets, so grab a jar and give it a try – it's not too hot, but packed with flavour. (You'll also need harissa paste for the Harissa haddock stew with chickpeas, page 138.)

SERVES 4 AS A SIDE

TOOLS: SMALL SAUCEPAN (FOR MELTED BUTTER) | SPOON | BASTING BRUSH | CHOPPING KNIFE | CHOPPING BOARD | SERVING PLATE

4 whole mealies (corn on the cob)
60–90 ml (4–6 Tbsp) butter
30 ml (2 Tbsp) harissa paste
salt and pepper, to taste
a small bunch spring onions, finely sliced (optional)
a handful fresh coriander, finely chopped (optional)

Strip away all the husks (leaf sheaths) and corn silk (threads) from the mealies (or tie the husks to the back to create a 'turning handle', if you like). Melt the butter in a saucepan and stir in the harissa paste. Season with salt and pepper, then brush the mealies on all sides with the mixture.

Grill over medium-hot coals until lightly charred and fragrant. Remove from the heat and brush generously with the remaining butter mixture. Transfer to a serving plate and, if using, sprinkle with spring onions and coriander, and serve immediately.

Roasted butternut
with tahini, nuts and herbs

Vegetables wrapped in foil and roasted directly over hot coals, is one of the most underrated ways of cooking (whether you're at home or in the middle of nowhere). It requires very little attention or effort, yet yields a charred outer with the most delicious steamed interior. I choose small butternuts for this recipe, and roast them in halves or quarters – this way the cut sides also colour beautifully.

SERVES 6 AS A SIDE

TOOLS: CHEF'S KNIFE OR CHOPPING KNIFE | CUTTING BOARD | FOIL | PREPARED FIRE WITH HOT COALS | SERVING PLATTER | SPOON FOR HONEY

3 baby/small butternuts, halved or quartered, seeds and pith removed
extra virgin olive oil, for drizzling
salt and pepper, to taste
5–10 ml (1–2 tsp) smoked paprika (optional)
30–45 ml (2–3 Tbsp) tahini
15 ml (1 Tbsp) fresh lemon juice
15–30 ml (1–2 Tbsp) water
15 ml (1 Tbsp) honey
a handful roasted salted mixed nuts, roughly chopped
a handful fresh herbs, finely chopped (e.g. parsley, dill, coriander, basil, mint)

Prepare a fire for hot coal roasting. Cut out six squares of foil (for butternut halves, or 12 if you're doing quarters) about 30 × 30 cm.

Place a butternut half or quarter in the middle of each foil square, drizzling well with olive oil and seasoning with salt, pepper and paprika. Wrap the butternut completely in the foil. When the coals are ready, place the wrapped butternut halves directly on the medium-hot coals (I usually place them on the sides of the prepared fire/coals, so that I can grill meat in the centre at the same time, if necessary). Turn the butternuts every 7–10 minutes, roasting until they are fully cooked and charred at the edges (it should take 20–30 minutes; open one carefully to check after 20 minutes). Remove from the fire, remove the foil and place cut sides-up on a serving platter. Place the tahini, lemon juice, honey, water (add just enough water for a pouring consistency) and a pinch of salt and pepper in a jar with a lid and shake until well mixed. Drizzle all over the butternuts, then top with chopped nuts and chopped herbs. Serve hot.

Note

- *For oven roasting, arrange the oiled, seasoned butternuts without foil on a baking tray and bake in a preheated oven at 220°C for 25–30 minutes, or until tender and slightly charred. Remove from the oven and serve as above.*

Polenta
with blue cheese and pan-fried mushrooms

Polenta is the Italian cousin of 'mieliepap', so technically you can serve polenta as a replacement for 'mieliepap', and vice versa. I love the yellow colour and smooth texture of polenta though, and when it's topped with something buttery and cheesy it becomes the stuff of my dreams. I can easily have this dish for dinner, served in individual wide bowls, but it's a stunning side dish to a deeply savoury and saucy stew (such as the Red wine-braised venison stew [page 174]), with or without the mushrooms.

SERVES 4 AS A SIDE

TOOLS: LARGE WIDE PAN | CHOPPING BOARD | CHOPPING KNIFE | SPATULA | MEDIUM POT | WIDE SERVING BOWL

60 ml (¼ cup) butter
400 g mixed mushrooms, roughly chopped
a handful fresh thyme, woody stalks discarded
salt and pepper, to taste
500 ml (2 cups) milk
500 ml (2 cups) chicken stock (1 stock cube dissolved in 500 ml boiling water)
250 ml (1 cup) fine polenta
125 ml (½ cup) grated parmesan
100 g blue cheese, crumbled

Melt the butter in a pan over medium-high heat and fry the mushrooms until lightly browned and soft (use a spatula), adding the thyme halfway through. Season generously with salt and pepper, then set aside while you make the polenta.

Pour the milk and stock into a pot and bring to a simmer. Add the polenta in a steady stream, stirring continuously to prevent lumps, then cook over medium-low heat until the polenta thickens (3–5 minutes), stirring very often to prevent the bottom from burning. When it is cooked, remove from the heat, season generously with salt and pepper and stir in the parmesan. Transfer to a serving bowl, top with the fried mushrooms (along with any remaining buttery juices in the pan) and scatter over the crumbled blue cheese. Garnish as desired and serve immediately.

Notes

- *There are different types of polenta, from fine to coarse. This recipe works best with the finest one.*

- *Polenta will continue to thicken on standing, so don't make it too far ahead. If needed, add a splash of very hot water and stir well to loosen before serving.*

Foil-roasted potatoes
with garlic and herb butter and sour cream

I almost didn't include this recipe, because people have been roasting potatoes in foil over fire since forever. But when a potato is good, it's EVERYTHING. And to me, the combination of the melted garlic and herb butter on the fluffy, slightly charred potato with added cool, thick sour cream is as good as it gets. Again, foil is your friend – just turn the potatoes every now and then so that they don't get completely blackened on one side only.

SERVES 6 AS A SIDE

TOOLS: MEDIUM BOWL | CHOPPING BOARD | CHOPPING KNIFE | FINE GRATER | FORK | FOIL | SCISSORS (OPTIONAL), SKEWER OR SHARP SMALL KNIFE

250 g softened butter
15 ml (1 Tbsp) extra virgin olive oil, plus extra
a handful fresh parsley and/or chives, finely chopped (reserve some for topping)
2 cloves garlic, finely grated
salt and pepper, to taste
6 large potatoes
250 g thick sour cream

Prepare a fire for making hot coals. Cut out six squares of foil, each about 25 × 25 cm.

To make the garlic and herb butter, place the butter, oil, herbs and garlic in a bowl, then season generously with salt and pepper. Use a fork to mash it all to a chunky texture, then set aside.

Prick each potato a few times with a fork, then place each on a square of foil. Drizzle lightly with oil and season with salt, rubbing with your hands to coat well. Wrap the potatoes tightly in the foil to cover completely and place directly on medium hot coals at the edges of the fire. Cook for about 1 hour, turning every 8–10 minutes. Carefully open one of the potatoes and insert a skewer or small sharp knife to test if its tender all the way through. If necessary, return to the coals and cook for another 10 minutes until cooked. Remove from the fire, then open the foil. Slice a cross on top of each potato, press the sides gently to reveal the soft inner, then top generously with a tablespoon of the herb butter (it will melt quickly), and serve with dollops of sour cream and a sprinkle of chopped parsley and chives.

Note

- If you want to roast potatoes in the oven instead of over a fire, do it without foil. Place them on a baking tray, prick lightly and cover them in olive oil and salt, then roast at 180°C for 1 hour. Serve as above.

Sandwiches

Party-size caprese sandwich

The winning combination of ripe tomato, soft mozzarella and basil remains one of the greatest loves of my life. Turn a fresh ciabatta into a delightful sandwich that can be sliced up for your picnic, a quick lunch or even a warm toasted side dish (braaibroodjie-style) on the fire.

SERVES 4–6 AS A SNACK

TOOLS: CUTTING BOARD | BREAD KNIFE | SPREADING KNIFE | SLICING KNIFE

1 fresh wood-fired ciabatta loaf (or other similar loaf of your choice)
butter, for spreading
2 × 100 g balls fior di latte, sliced
±125 ml (½ cup) drained and roughly chopped marinated sun-dried tomatoes

2 large ripe tomatoes, thinly sliced
salt and pepper, to taste
a handful fresh basil or rocket leaves
a few Tbsp store-bought basil pesto

Using a bread knife, slice the ciabatta loaf horizontally and spread the cut sides with butter. Over the lower half of the loaf, arrange the fior di latte in a generous layer, followed by sun-dried tomatoes, fresh tomatoes and some salt and pepper. Top with basil or rocket. Spread the upper half of the loaf with pesto and close the loaf (so that it appears 'whole' again), pressing down gently to compress slightly. On a cutting board, carefully slice the loaf (the 'sandwich') into portions. Serve immediately, or wrap individually in wax paper and pack into your picnic basket.

For braaibroodjie-style serving, don't slice the sandwich yet – place it in a hinged grid, then braai over medium to low heat coals, turning often, until the outside is toasted and the cheese has fully melted. Transfer to a cutting board, slice and serve hot.

Notes

- *Marinated sun-dried tomatoes are readily available at many supermarkets. If you can't find them, look for something like marinated roasted tomatoes, in the antipasti section.*

- *For a more economical version, use 2 cups roughly grated regular mozzarella cheese instead of fior di latte.*

Spicy cauliflower tacos

with guacamole, tomato and coriander

Gone are the days of drab, boiled cauliflower, now that we know how fabulous it can be when charred or fried! These little nuggets are incredibly tasty and they make a fantastic filling for tacos, but you can also serve them on top of a creamy cabbage slaw with sliced avocado. For an extra toasty exterior, fry them in enough oil to coat the bottom of the pan in a thin layer, then drain on kitchen paper before serving.

SERVES 6 AS A LIGHT MEAL

TOOLS: SMALL MIXING BOWL | TEASPOON | LARGE WIDE PAN | SPATULA | SLOTTED SPOON | BOWL | CHOPPING BOARD | CHOPPING KNIFE

5 ml (1 tsp) smoked paprika

5 ml (1 tsp) curry powder

5 ml (1 tsp) ground cumin

2.5 ml (½ tsp) chilli powder (optional)

5 ml (1 tsp) salt

freshly ground black pepper, to taste

60 ml (¼ cup) vegetable oil

1 medium head cauliflower, sliced into small florets

6–12 corn tortillas (crisp or soft, or any flour tortillas of your choice, page 17)

3 cups (750 ml) shredded lettuce

1–2 large tomatoes, diced (or Sweet and spicy tomato and red pepper salsa [page 40])

1 batch Yoghurt guacamole (page 39), or 1 freshly smashed avocado

250 ml (1 cup) sour cream

a handful fresh coriander, roughly chopped

In a bowl, combine the spices, salt and a grinding of pepper, then stir to mix and set aside. Heat the oil in a pan and fry the florets over medium-high heat until golden brown, working in batches. Remove with a slotted spoon and drain on kitchen paper. Transfer to a bowl and season generously on all sides with the spice mix.

To serve, toast the tortillas briefly over medium heat (optional), then fill with lettuce, tomatoes, guacamole, fried cauliflower, some sour cream and fresh coriander. Garnish as desired.

Chicken-mayo rolls
with celery, apple, walnuts and dill

Chicken-mayonnaise has always been my first choice sandwich filling. Fresh or toasted, on white or wholewheat, in wraps or on bagels – any bread will do. For a picnic, I prefer an individual roll to a sliced bread sandwich – it just holds together better. This chicken-mayo filling might look familiar; it's a spin on a traditional Waldorf salad in a generous chicken sandwich format. The filling and sandwiches can be made with store-bought rotisserie chicken a day ahead – just cover or wrap and refrigerate. Creamy, crunchy, nutty and fresh all wrapped into one.

MAKES 8 SMALL-MEDIUM SANDWICHES

TOOLS: MEDIUM TO LARGE MIXING BOWL | SPOON | CHOPPING BOARD | CHOPPING KNIFE | BREAD KNIFE OR SERRATED KNIFE | SPREADING KNIFE

125 ml (½ cup) good quality mayonnaise
125 ml (½ cup) double cream plain yoghurt
15–30 ml (1–2 Tbsp) fresh lemon juice
2 celery stalks, finely chopped
1 unpeeled green apple, cored and finely diced
50 g (½ cup) walnuts, roughly chopped
a handful fresh dill, roughly chopped
salt and pepper, to taste
1 medium rotisserie chicken, deboned and roughly chopped or shredded
8 small-medium (or 6 medium-large) white or wholewheat fresh rolls
butter, for spreading
a handful fresh lettuce leaves

Combine the mayonnaise, yoghurt, lemon juice, celery, apple, walnuts and dill in a mixing bowl. Season generously with salt and pepper. Mix well then add the chicken and stir to mix. Slice each roll in half horizontally, spread with butter, top with a generous amount of the chicken mixture and a few lettuce leaves (or whatever order you prefer), then close the roll. Serve immediately, or store in an airtight container in the fridge (for up to a day) until ready to serve. Alternatively, wrap the filled rolls individually in wax paper or baking paper, and pack for a picnic.

Note

- *Choose a soft roll that is easy to bite into (coney rolls won't work for this because of their crispy crusts, but any burger bun or wholewheat roll will do the trick).*

Chicken tikka tortillas *with lime yoghurt, quick-pickled cucumber and nutty seeds*

These scrumptious tortillas are made with the help of a few store-bought essentials, such as tikka marinade and nutty seed salad sprinkle. If you like, however, you could make your own tortilla wraps (page 17). Quick-pickled cucumbers only take a few minutes to put together, so make them first and leave them to steep while you complete the rest. The combination is spicy, savoury, saucy, crunchy and super delicious.

SERVES 4–6

TOOLS: LARGE GLASS JAR (500 G CAPACITY) OR CERAMIC BOWL | CUP MEASURE | CHOPPING BOARD | CHOPPING KNIFE | TABLESPOON | SMALL MIXING BOWL | FINE GRATER | LARGE PAN AND HEAT SOURCE | SPATULA OR WOODEN SPOON | PAN FOR DRY-TOASTING TORTILLAS

FOR THE QUICK-PICKLED CUCUMBER
125 ml (½ cup) water
125 ml (½ cup) white vinegar or cider vinegar
30 ml (2 Tbsp) sugar
5 ml (1 tsp) mustard seeds (optional)
½ large cucumber, finely sliced

FOR THE TORTILLAS
250 ml (1 cup) double cream plain yoghurt
zest and juice of 2 limes
30 ml (2 Tbsp) vegetable oil
600 g chicken breasts, sliced into bite-size chunks
250 ml (1 cup) chicken tikka marinade/sauce
salt and pepper, to taste
4–6 large tortilla wraps, lightly toasted
1 batch Yoghurt guacamole (page 39) (optional)
1 small red cabbage, finely sliced or shredded
± 35 g nut and seed sprinkle for salads (optional)
a handful fresh coriander, roughly chopped

First make the quick-pickled cucumber. Mix the water, vinegar, sugar and mustard seeds (if using) together in a jar or ceramic mixing bowl. Add the cucumber and leave to pickle for at least 30 minutes before using, or cover and refrigerate overnight.

To prepare the lime yoghurt, stir the yoghurt, lime zest and juice together in a small mixing bowl. Refrigerate until ready to serve.

For the chicken tortillas, heat the oil in a pan over medium heat, then add the chicken. Fry for about 3 minutes until lightly golden, then add the tikka marinade and stir, heating through. Turn down the heat to low and simmer for about 5 minutes, seasoning with salt and pepper. Remove from the heat when the chicken is cooked.

To assemble, place a toasted tortilla on a plate, spread with a little guacamole (if using), then top with cabbage, a generous amount of quick-pickled cucumber, some of the saucy tikka chicken, and a swirl of lime yoghurt. Finish with nut and seed sprinkle (if using) and fresh coriander, fold and serve warm.

Falafel burgers
with guacamole, tomato and rocket

We know that vegetable-based burgers are a clever, sustainable choice, but they're also utterly delicious and need to be on your menu at least once a month. As mentioned in my recipe for Spiced falafel balls with crispy curry leaves (page 74), I choose to keep it simple and use a convenient store-bought falafel premix for the chickpea patties – it just needs water to come together. Take them to the next level with the addition of some fresh herbs and garlic, a few dried spices, ripe tomatoes, creamy guacamole and peppery rocket leaves. Keep it completely vegan by toasting the cut side of the buns with a drizzle of extra virgin olive oil (or butter if you prefer), before assembly.

SERVES 4

TOOLS: GRATER | MEDIUM MIXING BOWL | CUTTING BOARD | CHOPPING KNIFE | SPOON | NON-STICK BAKING PAPER | PLATE OR TRAY | SERRATED KNIFE | NON-STICK FRYING PAN | SPATULA

1 × 200 g packet falafel premix
5–10 ml (1–2 tsp) braai spice
a handful fresh Italian parsley, finely chopped (optional)
2 cloves garlic, finely grated or chopped
200 ml (¾ cup) hot water
4 large burger buns
olive oil, for frying, plus extra
vegan mayonnaise (optional)
a small bunch fresh rocket or watercress
1 batch Yoghurt guacamole (page 39), or freshly mashed avocado
2 large tomatoes (red or green), sliced

Add the premix, spice, parsley, garlic and water to a mixing bowl, then mix to a stiff paste. Divide into four portions and shape into balls (work with wet hands to prevent sticking, if necessary). Gently flatten each ball with the palm of your hands to a diameter similar to the burger buns, then place each on a small square of non-stick baking paper and set them aside on a plate or tray (the paper makes them easier to handle).

Slice the buns in half horizontally, drizzle the cut sides lightly with oil, then fry the cut sides in a pan over medium heat until golden brown (work in batches). Set the buns aside, then add more oil to the pan and place the patties paper-side up in the pan, removing the paper. Fry the patties on both sides until golden brown and cooked. Remove from the heat.

To assemble, arrange the bottom halves of the toasted buns on plates, then top generously with mayonnaise (if using), rocket or watercress, fried patties, guacamole or avocado and sliced tomato. Close the burgers and serve immediately.

Grilled BBQ chicken and pineapple burgers *with brie and chutney*

I grew up in a home in which my parents loved fruit chutney in or on pretty much everything – meat marinades, stews, braaibroodjies, boerewors rolls, oxtail potjie, chicken tray bakes, gravy, you name it. I still love this taste of my childhood, but I use chutney a little more selectively now. With these scrumptious chicken burgers though, you can really be generous as chutney and brie are perfect partners. This one's for you, Mom and Dad!

SERVES 4

TOOLS: SERRATED KNIFE | SPREADING KNIFE | CHOPPING BOARD | MEAT HAMMER OR MALLET OR ROLLING PIN | SLICING KNIFE | PREPARED FIRE AND GRID (OR FRYING PAN WITH HEAT SOURCE) | TONGS | BASTING BRUSH

4 large burger buns
butter, for spreading
4 chicken breasts
salt and pepper, to taste
125 ml (½ cup) barbecue or braai marinade
4 slices pineapple (fresh or canned)
good quality mayonnaise, for spreading
a small bunch lettuce
2 tomatoes, sliced
125–250 g brie, sliced
125 ml (½ cup) fruit chutney of your choice

Slice the buns horizontally, spread them with butter and toast the buttered sides in a pan or over medium hot coals. Set aside.

On a chopping board and using a meat hammer or rolling pin, hammer the chicken breasts lightly until they are tender, of even thickness (they will shrink somewhat during cooking) and slightly wider than the buns. Season the chicken with salt and pepper, then grill them over medium-hot coals (or grill in a pan with a little olive oil), basting often with the barbecue marinade (they'll cook quickly). Remove from the heat, then grill or fry the pineapple on both sides until slightly charred. Remove from the heat and set aside.

To assemble, spread the bottom halves of the buns generously with mayonnaise, then top with lettuce, tomato, grilled chicken, sliced brie, grilled or fried pineapple and chutney. Close with the top halves and serve immediately.

When hammering chicken breasts, place the meat between two sheets of plastic to prevent it from sticking (remember to rinse and recycle the plastic afterwards).

Greek-style boerewors rolls
with yoghurt, mint and tomato salad

Everybody loves a boerewors roll – it's quick, easy and always delicious. Most of us use good old tomato sauce, or a homemade tomato and onion relish, but do try this Greek-inspired combo next time; it really puts a fresh spin on a very familiar favourite, especially if you have access to lamb boerewors.

SERVES 4

TOOLS: MEDIUM MIXING BOWL | CHOPPING BOARD | CHOPPING KNIFE | SPOON | SMALL MIXING BOWL | HOT COALS FOR GRILLING | SERRATED KNIFE | SPREADING KNIFE

2 large ripe tomatoes, diced or 12 baby tomatoes, sliced

250 ml (1 cup) finely diced cucumber

½ small red onion, finely sliced

a small bunch fresh mint, stalks discarded

15 ml (1 Tbsp) red wine vinegar

15 ml (1 Tbsp) extra virgin olive oil

salt and pepper, to taste

125 ml (½ cup) double cream plain yoghurt

±500 g lamb (or beef) boerewors

4 large fresh hotdog rolls

butter, for spreading

In a medium mixing bowl, combine the tomatoes, cucumber and red onion. On a chopping board, finely slice half of the mint leaves into thin shreds, then add them to the bowl. Add the vinegar and olive oil, and season with salt and pepper. Toss to mix and set aside.

Add the yoghurt to a small mixing bowl. Finely chop the remaining mint leaves (but reserve a few for garnishing) and add them to the yoghurt, along with some salt and pepper, and mix well.

Grill the boerewors over hot coals until golden brown but still juicy. Remove from the fire and cut into portions as long as the rolls. Slice open the rolls from the top lengthways (don't slice all the way through) and butter the cut sides. Top each bun with some tomato salad, a few dollops of minty yoghurt and a portion of grilled wors. Garnish with the reserved mint and serve immediately.

Note

- *If you have a blender handy, blend the yoghurt and mint together for a delicious speckled mint-yoghurt sauce.*

Ultimate classic beef burgers
with balsamic caramelised onions

Beef burgers can easily be mediocre. But with a few simple changes, home-made burgers will trump any artisanal burger-stand's or restaurant's offering. Take the effort out of making patties by choosing good quality ready-made from your local butchery or supermarket, then focus on the balsamic caramelised onions – they make a world of difference.

SERVES 4

TOOLS: CHOPPING BOARD | CHOPPING KNIFE | LARGE POT | WOODEN SPOON OR SPATULA | SMALL MIXING BOWL | SPOON | SERRATED KNIFE | SPREADING KNIFE | LARGE PAN WITH HEAT SOURCE OR HOT COALS WITH GRID | BASTING BRUSH | HEATPROOF SPATULA

30–45 ml (2–3 Tbsp) olive oil, plus extra

2 large onions, halved and thinly sliced into 'C' shapes

60 ml (¼ cup) balsamic vinegar

30 ml (2 Tbsp) dark brown sugar

salt and pepper, to taste

125 ml (½ cup) mayonnaise

30 ml (2 Tbsp) braai marinade or barbecue sauce, plus extra

10 ml (2 tsp) smoked paprika

4 large sesame burger buns

butter, for spreading

4 × 150–200 g best quality beef burger patties

4 large slices mature cheddar or gouda

4–8 crunchy lettuce leaves, shredded

1–2 ripe tomatoes, thinly sliced

a few pickled gherkins, thinly sliced

First make the balsamic caramelised onions. Heat the oil in a large pot over medium heat, then add the onions, breaking them up with a wooden spoon into individual strands. Continue frying and stirring for at least 15 minutes, until the onions become very soft and golden and a light brown stickiness starts to form at the bottom of the pot. Turn up the heat, then add the vinegar and sugar, stirring to loosen the sticky bits at the bottom. Season with salt and pepper, then continue to cook until the liquid has almost completely reduced. Remove from the heat and leave to cool.

For the burger mayo, mix the mayonnaise, braai marinade or barbecue sauce and smoked paprika together. Set aside.

Slice the buns open, butter the cut sides and give them a light toast in a pan or over medium-hot coals. Set aside.

Grill the patties over hot coals (or fry with some oil in a pan), basting with more braai marinade as you grill or fry. When almost done, place the cheese slices on top and leave to melt in the residual heat for a minute, then remove them from the grill or pan.

Spread the bottom halves of the buns with some mayo mix, then top with lettuce, tomato, cheese-topped patties, a generous helping of onions and gherkins. Replace the top halves of the toasted buns and serve at once.

Notes

- *Choose large, well-rounded, sesame-coated burger buns, and always toast the cut sides with butter.*

- *As most patties tend to shrink, use a plate and gentle pressure to flatten them a little wider than the buns before cooking, then they will be the same size as the bun when cooked.*

Picanha steak sandwich

with creamy wholegrain mustard and watercress

A picanha steak's fibres run lengthways (like a whole fillet), so when you slice it thinly after grilling, it's easier to bite through than most other steaks. I chose fresh paninis (small ciabattas) for this sandwich, because you need something a little sturdier than a burger roll, but less crusty than sourdough. This is a fabulous quick lunch solution, stretching any large steak to feed a group.

SERVES 4

TOOLS: PLATE | LARGE IRON SKILLET OR GRIDDLE WITH HEAT SOURCE (OR BRAAI FIRE WITH GRID) | TONGS | CHOPPING BOARD | SERRATED KNIFE | SPREADING KNIFE | SLICING KNIFE | SMALL MIXING BOWL | SPOON

600–800 g picanha steak
15–30 ml (1–2 Tbsp) extra virgin olive oil
salt and pepper, to taste
4 large panini rolls
butter, for spreading
aïoli or Cheat's truffle aïoli (page 32) or plain good quality mayonnaise, for spreading
a bunch fresh watercress or rocket leaves
2 large ripe tomatoes, sliced
a few pickled gherkins, finely sliced
15 ml (1 Tbsp) wholegrain mustard
125 ml (½ cup) sour cream

Place the steak on a plate, drizzle with olive oil on both sides and season with salt and pepper. Place an iron skillet or griddle over high heat, heating to smoking point, then grill the steak (without adding more oil to the skillet) on both sides for 4–5 minutes a side depending on the thickness of the meat; you're looking for a rare to medium-rare result. Remove from the skillet and leave to rest for about 8 minutes.

To assemble, slice the paninis open horizontally, spread with butter and give the cut sides a quick toast in the skillet. Spread the bottom halves generously with aïoli, then top with watercress, tomato slices and gherkin.

On a cutting board, slice the rested steak as thinly as possible, then top each sandwich generously with the slices. Season with salt and pepper.

Combine the mustard and sour cream in a mixing bowl, then spread the cut sides of the top halves generously and close the sandwiches. Serve at once, or cover and refrigerate until ready to serve (best served warm or at room temperature).

Notes

- *If you're not keen on aïoli, use regular mayonnaise, and if sour cream isn't your thing, spread the wholegrain mustard as is.*

- *Toasting the buttered sides of the bread takes a meat sandwich to new heights, but is not essential if you're pressed for time.*

- *You can also grill this steak over a fire on a grid.*

Fish &
seafood

Trout gravlax

If you're not familiar with gravlax (also known as gravadlax), it's an age-old Nordic way of curing fish (usually salmon) in salt and sugar, sometimes with the addition of herbs and/or spirits such as vodka. It is served thinly sliced with a mustard sauce, perhaps some rye or seeded bread and a green salad. All you need is really fresh fish, some patience (it takes at least a day), and a fridge. This recipe keeps it simple, using only salt, sugar and dill, and it makes an elegant, simple, light lunch.

SERVES 6

TOOLS: MEDIUM MIXING BOWL | CHOPPING BOARD | CHOPPING OR SLICING KNIFE | CLINGFILM | KITCHEN PAPER | TRAY OR CONTAINER FOR FRIDGE | FLAT PLATE OR BOARD PLUS 3 CANS OF FOOD (FOR WEIGHING DOWN) | FRIDGE | SMALL MIXING BOWL | TABLESPOON

250 ml (1 cup) coarse salt

250 ml (1 cup) regular white sugar

a handful fresh dill, finely chopped, plus extra

2 large (800–900 g in total) boneless rainbow trout fillets, skin-on (see Note)

black pepper, to taste

FOR THE MUSTARD SAUCE

250 ml (1 cup) sour cream

30 ml (2 Tbsp) wholegrain mustard

15 ml (1 Tbsp) Dijon mustard

15 ml (1 Tbsp) honey (optional)

Place the salt, sugar and dill in a medium bowl and stir to mix. Scatter a quarter of the salt mixture over a large piece of clingfilm. Rinse the fish fillets under cold water and pat them dry with kitchen paper. Place one fillet flesh-side up on the clingfilm, scatter over two-thirds of the remaining mixture, then place the second fillet on top, flesh-side down so that the thick part of the top fillet faces the thin part of the bottom fillet. Scatter over the remaining salt mixture, then wrap up tightly in the clingfilm. Place the package on a tray or container that will fit into your fridge. Position a smaller flat plate or board on top, weighing it down with a few cans of food. Refrigerate for 24 hours, turning the parcel over after 12 hours. The sugar and salt will draw liquid out of the salmon and turn into a sticky brine.

Unwrap the fish and rinse the curing mixture off under cold running water, then pat dry with kitchen paper. Place the fillets skin-side down on a cutting board, then slice the gravlax thinly on an angle off the skin.

For the mustard sauce, mix the sour cream, mustards and honey (if using) together.

Serve the gravlax with the sauce on the side, scattered with the extra fresh dill and a grinding of pepper. Store, covered, in the fridge for up to two days.

Notes

· Don't use fine table salt for this recipe; it will penetrate the fish too quickly and result in a very salty taste.

· If you can't find rainbow trout, you can also use ocean trout or salmon trout.

· Thinner fillets will need a shorter curing time than thick fillets – adjust accordingly.

· You can also use one large salmon fillet for this recipe, cured for 28–36 hours.

Seared tuna *with sesame and soy*

Also known as tuna tataki, this simple dish requires the freshest tuna and just a handful other ingredients. Incredibly flavourful yet light, it's one of those dishes that leaves me saying: 'I want to eat like this every day!'

SERVES 4

TOOLS: CUTTING BOARD | CHEF'S KNIFE | PLATE | WIDE PAN | SMALL MIXING BOWL OR CUP | FINE GRATER | SPOON | SERVING PLATTER OR PLATES

500–600 g very fresh tuna steak (flash-frozen is perfect, just thaw before cooking)
salt and pepper, to taste
60 ml (¼ cup) white and/or black sesame seeds
30 ml (2 Tbsp) extra virgin olive oil
60 ml (¼ cup) soy sauce
15 ml (1 Tbsp) rice vinegar (or lemon juice)
5 ml (1 tsp) sesame oil
30 ml (2 Tbsp) finely grated fresh ginger
a pinch chilli flakes (optional)
a small bunch spring onions, finely sliced

Season the tuna steak with salt and pepper. Sprinkle the sesame seeds on a plate, then dip the tuna to coat all sides with the seeds. Heat the oil in a pan and sear each steak for about 60 seconds per side, then remove from the pan and set aside to rest.

To make the sauce, combine the soy sauce, vinegar, sesame oil, ginger and chilli flakes (if using) and stir well.

Slice the tuna with a very sharp knife into 5 mm-thick slices, then arrange them on a platter (or individual plates). Spoon the sauce over, then top with spring onions. Serve at room temperature with salt and pepper on the side.

Be sure to choose sustainably caught tuna (try greenfish.co.za — they sell great quality flash-frozen tuna that works perfectly for this recipe), and follow the MSC initiative that promotes line-caught local tuna: one fisherman, one tuna.

Grilled yellowtail
with spiced apricot glaze

You can use this versatile glaze as a marinade for almost any type of fish, from snoek through yellowtail to trout. I love the smoky flavour that fire grilling adds, especially for large whole fillets, but you can certainly also cook smaller pieces of fish in a pan, and add the glaze towards the end of the cooking process. You'll need a hinged grid for turning the fish over – oil the inside of the grid as well as the skin side of the fish to prevent sticking.

SERVES 4

TOOLS: SMALL POT OR SAUCEPAN | WOODEN SPOON | FINE GRATER | CHOPPING BOARD | PREPARED FIRE AND CLEAN HINGED GRID | KITCHEN PAPER | BASTING BRUSH | LARGE SPATULA | SERVING PLATTER

125 ml (½ cup) butter
1–2 cloves garlic, finely grated
30 ml (2 Tbsp) finely grated fresh ginger
10 ml (2 tsp) smoked paprika
5 ml (1 tsp) ground cumin
30 ml (2 Tbsp) smooth apricot jam
grated rind and juice of 1 large lemon
salt and pepper, to taste
30–45 ml (2–3 Tbsp) vegetable oil
1 large (600–800 g) fresh fillet of fish, preferably pin-boned
a handful fresh dill or parsley, roughly chopped, for serving (optional)
lemon wedges, for serving

In a pot or saucepan, melt the butter over medium heat. Add the garlic, ginger, paprika, cumin, jam, lemon rind and juice then season lightly with salt and pepper. Bring to a simmer, stirring briefly until smooth, then remove the glaze from the heat.

Prepare your fire for grilling over medium-hot coals, and grease the inside of a clean hinged grid (use kitchen paper or a basting brush) with some of the vegetable oil. On a clean working surface, pat the fish dry with kitchen paper, then oil the skin side with vegetable oil and arrange on the grid. Baste the flesh side generously with the glaze, then close the grid and grill on the skin side for 10–15 minutes, or until the flesh starts turning opaque in places (as the fish cooks from the skin side through). Turn the fish over to grill on the flesh side for just a few minutes to give it colour, then turn over again and baste generously with the glaze. Remove from the grid using a large spatula, transfer to a serving platter and serve hot (scattered with herbs if you're using), with lemon wedges and your choice of sides and/or a salad.

Harissa haddock stew
with chickpeas

This simple and tasty one-pan stew comes together in minutes, and is made with a few pantry staples and some frozen haddock – I love the smoky flavour that it brings. Of course you can also use fresh fish fillets or even a mixture of seafood of your choice; it will just have a fresher end result without the smokiness. Serve with crusty bread or rice or some herbed couscous.

SERVES 4 AS A LIGHT MEAL

TOOLS: WIDE PAN OR CASSEROLE WITH HEAT SOURCE | FINE GRATER | CHOPPING BOARD | CHOPPING KNIFE | TABLESPOON | SPATULA OR WOODEN SPOON | JUG FOR STOCK | CUP MEASURE

45 ml (3 Tbsp) extra virgin olive oil
2–3 cloves garlic, finely grated
30 ml (2 Tbsp) harissa paste
30 ml (2 Tbsp) tomato paste
1 × 400 g can chickpeas, drained
250 ml (1 cup) chicken or vegetable stock
1 × 400 g can chopped tomatoes
5 ml (1 tsp) sugar
salt and pepper, to taste
400 g haddock fillets, sliced into bite-size chunks
125 ml (½ cup) plain double cream or low fat plain yoghurt
a handful fresh herbs, roughly chopped (e.g. dill, parsley, coriander)

Heat the olive oil in a pan or casserole over medium heat. Add the garlic, harissa paste and tomato paste, then give it a quick stir (just a few seconds). Add the chickpeas and continue to fry for about 3 minutes. Add the stock, canned tomatoes, sugar, salt and pepper, then stir and bring to a simmer. Cook for 2 minutes, then add the haddock and cook for another 3–5 minutes or until the fish is just cooked through. Remove from the heat and stir through the yoghurt. Top with the fresh herbs and serve warm (see serving suggestions above).

Coconut kingklip curry
with cardamom and curry leaves

This delicious fish curry is mild and incredibly fragrant. Curry leaves and cardamom are my secret weapons here – they create all the magic. There simply isn't a substitute for fresh curry leaves in my opinion, so if you can't find them in a shop, ask around if anyone has a tree at home.

SERVES 4

TOOLS: CHOPPING BOARD | CHOPPING KNIFE | FINE GRATER | LARGE HEAVY-BASED POT WITH LID | WOODEN SPOON | TEASPOON | TABLESPOON | PESTLE AND MORTAR | CAN OPENER

30 ml (2 Tbsp) vegetable oil (I use canola)

2 onions, finely chopped

45 ml (3 Tbsp) finely grated/chopped fresh ginger

3 cloves garlic, finely grated/chopped

±20 fresh curry leaves

30 ml (2 Tbsp) mild curry powder or roasted garam masala

seeds from 6–8 cardamom pods, pounded with a pestle and mortar and husks removed

15 ml (1 Tbsp) ground fennel (barishap)

10 ml (2 tsp) ground coriander

5 ml (1 tsp) ground turmeric

2.5 ml (½ tsp) chilli flakes (optional)

30 ml (2 Tbsp) tomato paste

1 × 400 g can chopped tomatoes

1 × 400 ml can coconut cream

salt and freshly ground black pepper, to taste

800 g–1 kg skinless boneless kingklip (or any firm white fish) fillets, cut into bite-size cubes

cooked jasmine or basmati rice, for serving

fresh coriander, for garnishing

flaked almonds and/or black sesame seeds, for garnishing

Heat the oil in a pot over medium heat and fry the onions until translucent (not brown). Add the ginger, garlic and curry leaves, and fry for 1 minute. Add the curry powder, cardamom, fennel, coriander, turmeric and chilli, then fry for another minute. The bottom of the pot will become quite dry at this point. Add the tomato paste and canned tomatoes and stir well. Pour in the coconut cream, stir and bring to a simmer, turning down the heat. Simmer for about 5 minutes, still stirring, then season well with salt and pepper. Add the fish cubes, stirring gently to cover them in sauce. Cover the pot and simmer for 10 minutes over low heat. Remove from the heat and serve in bowls with freshly cooked rice, all garnished with coriander leaves, flaked almonds and/or sesame seeds.

Notes

- *Order fresh or frozen fish such as kingklip via greenfish.co.za or the Abalobi app (depending on availability), and it will be delivered straight to your door.*

- *The husks of cardamom pods should be removed before serving as they are not pleasant to bite into.*

- *Curry leaves are not related to curry powder – they're green leaves from the South Indian curry tree, with a distinctive lemongrass-like flavour.*

Smoky chorizo rice
with mussels and tomato

This easy, flavoursome dish is based on one of Phillippa Cheifitz's recipes from her 2017 book, Make It Easy –
a simplified paella-style rice dish, originally made with calamari. Phillippa is the South African queen of simplicity
and so many of my recipes (and much of my food career) are inspired by her effortless ideas. I made this recipe
with fresh mussels in the shell, but you can substitute it with frozen mussels (available in the frozen seafood section
of many supermarkets) – just give them a quick blanch before you add them.

SERVES 4–6

TOOLS: COLANDER | CLEAN CLOTH | PARING KNIFE | CHOPPING BOARD | CHOPPING KNIFE | FINE GRATER | DEEP
30 CM-DIAMETER PAN OR HEAVY-BASED CASSEROLE DISH WITH HEAT SOURCE (AND LID OR FOIL) | WOODEN SPOON OR
SPATULA | MEASURING JUG FOR STOCK | CAN OPENER

1 kg fresh black mussels in shell (thawed if frozen)
200 g smoked cured chorizo
45 ml (3 Tbsp) extra virgin olive oil
1 onion, finely chopped
2–3 cloves garlic, finely grated
10 ml (2 tsp) smoked paprika
400 g uncooked risotto rice or sushi rice
750 ml (3 cups) chicken stock
1 × 400 g can chopped tomatoes
salt and pepper, to taste
a handful fresh Italian parsley, finely chopped
a few lemon wedges, for serving

Rinse the mussel meat in a colander under cold running water, then pat dry with a clean cloth and
set aside.

Using a sharp knife, make a slit down the side of the chorizo and remove the skin (as well as you can), then
slice into thin half-moons and set aside.

Heat the oil in a pan or casserole dish over high heat until it starts to simmer. Add the mussel meat (work
in two batches if necessary) and fry for 2–3 minutes until just cooked, then remove it from the pan. Turn the
heat down to medium, then add the onion and chorizo, frying until the onion is very soft and the chorizo
turns dark. Add the garlic and paprika and stir for 30 seconds, then add the rice, stock and tomatoes. Keep
stirring until it starts to simmer. Turn down the heat to low, cover with a lid and cook for about 15 minutes
until the rice is al dente tender but with a gentle bite. Add the fried mussel meat and stir gently. Remove
from the heat and season lightly with salt and pepper. Garnish with the parsley and serve immediately, with
some lemon wedges on the side.

Creamy tomato seafood soup

(cheat's bisque)

I used to make a longer version of this creamy tomato seafood soup for many years every December at Keurboomstrand, using fresh fish, fresh black mussels and whole prawns, as well as a seafood stock made from scratch. Although it's incredibly delicious, it is very time consuming. Since then I've come up with a much shorter method that is do-able year-round, using flash-frozen seafood (available in most supermarkets) and a few other tricks to deliver an easy, almost bisque-style seafood soup that will make you lick your bowl. A dash of brandy rounds it off perfectly. And don't be put off by the seemingly long list of ingredients; it's all simple stuff!

SERVES 4–6

TOOLS: CHOPPING BOARD | COARSE GRATER | FINE GRATER | CUP MEASURE | TABLESPOON | TEASPOON | LARGE POT WITH LID | WOODEN SPOON | SPATULA | CHOPPING KNIFE | LADLE

45 ml (3 Tbsp) extra virgin olive oil

½ onion, roughly grated

1 small carrot, finely grated

2 cloves garlic, finely grated

125 ml (½ cup) dry white wine

680 g smooth tomato passata (passata di pomodoro) (see Note)

250 ml (1 cup) chicken or fish stock (made from stock cubes/concentrate)

15 ml (1 Tbsp) Asian-style fish sauce (see Note)

10 ml (2 tsp) smoked paprika

400 g frozen prawns, thawed and cleaned of digestive tracts

400 g frozen boneless white fish fillets, thawed and cubed

300 g frozen mussel meat or mussels with shell, thawed

125–250 ml (½–1 cup) fresh cream, to taste

30 ml (2 Tbsp) brandy (optional)

salt and pepper, to taste

a handful fresh Italian parsley, finely chopped, for serving

crusty bread, for serving (optional)

In a large pot, heat the oil, then fry the onion, carrot and garlic over medium heat for 3–4 minutes, stirring often. Pour in the wine and turn the heat up, stirring, allowing it to reduce by half. Add the passata, stock, fish sauce and paprika, then bring to a simmer, still stirring. Turn the heat down to a slow simmer for 15 minutes and cover the pot partially with a lid.

Add the prawns, fish and mussel meat to the soup and simmer for 10 minutes until the seafood is just cooked. Stir in the cream and brandy (if using), bring to a simmer, then season generously with salt and pepper. Ladle into bowls, top with a final swirl of cream (ideally) and a sprinkle of parsley. Serve hot with bread, for dipping.

Notes

- Tomato passata is smooth, puréed, preserved tomatoes without skins or seeds, sold in glass bottles. Don't confuse it with canned tomato purée which is much more concentrated.

- Asian-style fish sauce brings some much-needed seafood umami depth in the absence of freshly made seafood stock, but you can leave it out if you don't have access to it.

- I had access to fresh black mussels for the accompanying photo, but frozen mussel meat or half shell mussels will work just as well.

Pan-fried prawn linguini

with garlic, paprika and lemon

I adore prawns and prepare them in many different ways, but this simple, creamy pasta brings all the luxurious feels with none of the effort. In case you didn't know, most of the flavour comes from the heads of the prawns, so keep them intact right until the end. It makes for a messy eating affair, but I don't mind that at all! Any true prawn lover will agree.

SERVES 4

TOOLS: COLANDER | RUNNING WATER | KITCHEN SCISSORS | FORK | EXTRA-LARGE WIDE PAN WITH HEAT SOURCE | LARGE POT | SPATULA | FINE GRATER | KNIFE | CHOPPING BOARD | LARGE POT WITH WATER FOR COOKING PASTA

800 g frozen whole King prawns
30 ml (2 Tbsp) extra virgin olive oil
60 ml (¼ cup) butter, plus extra
10 ml (2 tsp) smoked paprika
2 cloves garlic, finely grated or chopped
finely grated rind and juice of 1 medium lemon
250 ml (1 cup) cream
salt and pepper, to taste
400 g linguini pasta, freshly cooked
a handful fresh Italian parsley, finely chopped, for serving
fresh lemon wedges, for serving

Remove the packaging from the frozen prawns. Place them in a colander and run them under running, room-temperature water to thaw the outer icy layer quickly. They will start to separate from one another; continue until they are completely separated, then leave in the colander in a cool place to thaw completely (about 30 minutes). To clean the prawns, use kitchen scissors to cut from the top of the back (just behind the head) all the way to the end of the tail. Lift out the digestive tract with a fork and discard – this also makes the prawns very easy to shell while eating.

Heat the oil and half the butter in a very big pan or casserole, then stir in the paprika. Add the prawns, frying on one side until lightly brown. Turn them over, add the garlic and lemon rind and stir gently, until the prawns are lightly brown on both sides. Add the cream and bring to a simmer. Season with salt and pepper and keep simmering over low heat for 5 minutes, then add the freshly cooked pasta and stir through. Remove from the heat and add the lemon juice. Scatter with parsley. Serve warm from the pan, with some lemon wedges on the side (and plenty of paper napkins).

Notes

- *Boxes of whole prawns are available in the frozen seafood section of most supermarkets.*

- *Don't forget to look out for a trusted 'sustainably caught/farmed' sign when you buy prawns.*

Grilled seafood platter *with zesty salsa*

As with some other recipes in this book, this is more of a serving suggestion than a recipe, because it's just so simple. Choose your seafood according to what's available in your area, then grill it over high heat (over a grid or in a griddle pan), and as soon as it comes off the heat, drizzle it all over with this zippy, crunchy salsa. It's such a fresh way to enjoy seafood! Another great idea is to serve some Chunky tartare on the side (page 31).

SERVES 4

TOOLS: MEDIUM MIXING BOWL | TABLESPOON | CHOPPING BOARD | CHOPPING KNIFE | LARGE MIXING BOWL | PREPARED FIRE WITH GRID OR PERFORATED PAN (OR GRIDDLE PAN WITH HEAT SOURCE) | TONGS | SERVING PLATTER

80 ml (⅓ cup) extra virgin olive oil
45 ml (3 Tbsp) fresh lemon juice
a handful fresh Italian parsley, finely chopped
a handful fresh dill, finely chopped
1 bird's eye chilli, finely chopped, with seeds or scraped out (the seeds will increase the heat)
15 ml (1 Tbsp) finely chopped capers
a handful walnuts, finely chopped
salt and pepper, to taste
1–1.5 kg combination fresh seafood (e.g. fish, prawns, mussels, calamari tubes, crab, lobster, scallops)
fresh lemon wedges, for serving

In a medium mixing bowl, mix together the oil, lemon juice, parsley, dill, chilli, capers, walnuts and seasoning, then set aside.

Cut the fish into smaller portions, then add all the seafood to a large mixing bowl. Spoon half the salsa over the mixture and toss to coat. Grill over medium-hot coals or on a hot griddle for a few minutes until just cooked, removing with tongs and placing on a platter. Spoon the remaining salsa over, then serve with lemon wedges, ideally some crusty bread and your choice of sides or salads.

Chicken

Thai curry chicken sosaties

with coconut peanut sauce

These sosaties will leave you licking your fingers, especially because of the peanut sauce (which is good on almost everything). I usually prefer boneless thighs for chicken skewers, but in this case breast meat tends to be more resilient on the grid in terms of holding together. Use whatever you prefer.

SERVES 4

TOOLS: AT LEAST 8 SHORT TO MEDIUM BAMBOO SKEWERS | RECTANGULAR CONTAINER WITH LID | MIXING BOWL | CHOPPING BOARD | FINE GRATER | CHOPPING KNIFE | SMALL POT OR SAUCEPAN | WOODEN SPOON OR HAND WHISK | CUP MEASURE | TABLESPOON | HOT COALS WITH GRID

600 g boneless chicken breast or thighs, cubed
a handful fresh coriander, roughly chopped, for serving
black sesame seeds, for serving

FOR THE MARINADE
½ × 400 ml can coconut milk (shake before opening)
30 ml (2 Tbsp) red curry paste
30 ml (2 Tbsp) vegetable oil
15 ml (1 Tbsp) fish sauce
15 ml (1 Tbsp) finely grated fresh ginger
1 clove garlic, finely grated

zest 2 limes, finely grated
salt and pepper, to taste

FOR THE COCONUT PEANUT SAUCE
½ × 400 ml can coconut milk
60 ml (¼ cup) smooth peanut butter
60 ml (¼ cup) packed dark brown sugar
60 ml (¼ cup) soy sauce
30 ml (2 Tbsp) red curry paste
juice of 2 limes

Thread the chicken cubes onto skewers and place them in a rectangular container. Pour half a can of coconut milk into a mixing bowl, along with the curry paste, oil, fish sauce, ginger, garlic and lime zest. Season with salt and pepper, mix well and pour over the sosaties. Cover and refrigerate while you prepare the sauce (see Note).

For the coconut peanut sauce, place the remaining half-can of coconut milk, peanut butter, sugar, soy sauce and curry paste in a pot or saucepan. Bring to a simmer over medium heat, stirring until smooth and fully heated. Remove from the heat, stir in the lime juice and set aside to cool.

Grill the marinated sosaties over medium-hot coals until just cooked and golden brown, then remove from the heat. Drizzle over the peanut sauce and scatter with sesame seed and coriander leaves. Serve with a shredded cabbage salad (page 86) on the side. The sauce also makes a great salad dressing.

Notes

- *The sosaties may be marinated in the fridge up to one day before cooking.*

- *Try an alternative way to serve this dish: slice the chicken for stir-frying, then marinate the strips (without the oil). Drain the marinade, give the meat a quick stir-fry in some oil, then serve over noodles or rice or vegetables, drizzled with the peanut sauce and scattered with coriander.*

Miso-glazed chicken espetadas

I originally created the recipe for this four-ingredient miso glaze for my friends Riette and Henry at Pilgrim Wines; it takes only 5 minutes to prepare and is absolutely scrumptious on chicken, fish, vegetables, you name it. Boneless chicken drumsticks and/or thighs create generous espetadas (for sharing) on long metal skewers – elegant enough for your next dinner party, yet easy enough for any day of the week. Serve with the Charred broccoli and pak choy (page 98) or the Gem lettuce, avocado and blue cheese salad with ranch dressing (page 89).

SERVES 6

TOOLS: SMALL SAUCEPAN | WOODEN SPOON | AT LEAST 6 EXTRA-LONG SKEWERS | LARGE TRAY OR PLATE | BASTING BRUSH | BRAAI FIRE/HOT COALS | CUTTING BOARD AND CHOPPING KNIFE

45 ml (3 Tbsp) yellow or white miso paste
60 ml (¼ cup) good quality soy sauce
80 ml (⅓ cup) dry white wine
30 ml (2 Tbsp) muscovado or demerara sugar
±2 kg boneless chicken thighs or drumsticks
a small bunch spring onions, finely sliced, for serving
sliced radish, for serving

Add the miso paste, soy sauce, wine and sugar to a saucepan over low heat. Stir until the sugar and the paste have dissolved, then simmer the glaze for 2–3 minutes and remove from the heat.

Meanwhile, thread the chicken (fold each piece as you thread it) onto skewers. Arrange them on a tray or plate, then use a basting brush to coat generously with the glaze. Grill over medium-hot coals for 15–20 minutes, turning often and basting every few minutes, until just cooked (test one of the thickest centre pieces). Remove from the fire. Serve warm, sprinkled with sliced spring onions and radish slices, and your choice of sides or salad.

Easy sticky chutney chicken

Many South Africans of my generation grew up with a version of this recipe in the 1980s and '90s – chicken pieces smothered in a thick, sweet and savoury chutney and mayonnaise-based marinade, baked until shiny and sticky. It was one of our family's weekend favourites, baked and served over rice. My parents also prepared this on the braai, but because of the sugar content in the chutney, the sauce tended to burn easily. So they precooked the chicken pieces in the sauce, then finished them off over the fire to caramelise, reserving the cooking sauce for serving on the side. Totally old school, but finger-licking fantastic for the whole family. This is my adapted rendition of the retro classic.

SERVES 4–6

TOOLS: MIXING BOWL | CUP MEASURE | TABLESPOON | FINE GRATER | COARSE GRATER | CHOPPING BOARD | LARGE POT WITH LID | TONGS | HINGED GRID AND BRAAI FIRE OR KETTLE BRAAI OR LARGE BAKING OR CASSEROLE DISH AND OVEN

160 ml (⅔ cup) mild fruit chutney (or your favourite, mild or spicy)
160 ml (⅔ cup) mayonnaise
125 ml (½ cup) tomato sauce
60 ml (¼ cup) soy sauce
30 ml (2 Tbsp) Worcestershire sauce
2–3 cloves garlic, finely grated
1 medium onion, coarsely grated
12 mixed chicken pieces, bone-in
a handful fresh coriander, roughly chopped, for serving (optional)

To make the chutney marinade, add the chutney, mayo, tomato sauce, soy sauce, Worcestershire sauce, garlic and onion to a medium mixing bowl and stir to mix.

FOR COOKING ON A GRID OVER A FIRE: Add the marinade to a large pot and stir. Add the chicken pieces and stir to coat, then place over medium heat and bring to a simmer. Cook for about 40 minutes over low heat, partially covered with a lid, then remove the chicken pieces from the sauce using tongs. Using a hinged grid over medium-hot coals, braai the chicken pieces on both sides until browned and sticky (about 10 minutes only as these are cooked already), basting often with the remaining sauce. *Serve hot, garnished with fresh coriander, with the sauce on the side and your choice of sides (rice, potatoes, polenta, pap, salad, bread).

FOR COOKING IN A KETTLE BRAAI: Baste the raw chicken pieces generously with the marinade to coat them on all sides, then braai over indirect heat in the kettle braai, with the lid closed (vents open), for 45–50 minutes. The chicken is ready when it falls off the bone easily. Serve hot, as above*.

FOR COOKING IN THE OVEN: Preheat the oven to 180°C. Arrange the raw chicken pieces in a single layer in a baking or casserole dish, then pour the marinade sauce over, giving the dish a gentle shake to ensure the sauce is in all the crevices. Bake on the middle shelf for 60–75 minutes, or until brown all over (the meat should easily fall off the bone), then serve hot, as above*.

Note

· *As a variation on the classic version, try a different-flavoured chutney, such as dhania, jalapeño, Peppadew or mango.*

Smashed grilled chicken caprese

If it was up to me, I'd eat caprese salad every day – that classic Italian combo of milky fior di latte (fresh cow's milk mozzarella cheese), ripe tomatoes and punchy basil that's simple perfection. For those who prefer their lunches or dinners a little meatier, this double-protein, low-carb version will tick all the boxes. A store-bought pesto will save the day too, so you can prepare this meal without the use of a blender. Smashed chicken (pounded and tenderised) cooks in minutes and makes a neat stacking partner for the colourful, sliced salad. Interesting fact: Mozzarella cheese contains almost the same amount of protein as lean chicken breast.

SERVES 4

TOOLS: CLINGFILM | MEAT HAMMER OR ROLLING PIN (FOR POUNDING) | NON-STICK PAN | CHOPPING BOARD | CHEF'S KNIFE | TEASPOON | SERVING PLATE OR PLATTER

4 skinless chicken breasts
±45 ml (3 Tbsp) extra virgin olive oil, plus extra
salt and pepper, to taste
3 large or 4 medium ripe tomatoes, sliced
250–300 g fior di latte or buffalo mozzarella
60 ml (¼ cup) basil pesto
a handful fresh basil, for serving (optional)

Place the chicken breasts between sheets of clingfilm and pound with a meat hammer or rolling pin to a thickness of about 7 mm. Heat the oil in a non-stick pan over medium heat, then fry the pounded chicken on both sides until golden and just cooked. Season with salt and pepper. Remove from the heat and arrange on a plate or platter with sliced tomatoes and sliced mozzarella. Drizzle all over with pesto and scatter with fresh basil (if using), then serve immediately.

To take store-bought pesto to a drizzle-consistency, stir in some extra virgin olive oil.

Italian chicken stew
with aubergine, tomato and green olives

This simple, hearty chicken stew brings all the flavours of Sicily to your table in one pot. A handful of parmesan, fresh basil and a final drizzle of extra virgin olive oil will make everyone happy, but for that extra special celebration, top it with some roasted pine nuts. Serve with fluffy lemon and herb couscous, freshly cooked pasta, Polenta with blue cheese and pan-fried mushrooms (page 106), crusty ciabatta, or Quick-griddled yoghurt flatbreads (page 13).

SERVES 4

TOOLS: LARGE HEAVY-BASED POT (28–30 CM DIAMETER) WITH LID AND HEAT SOURCE OR MEDIUM-SIZE CAST-IRON POTJIE WITH STAND AND OPEN FIRE | TONGS | WOODEN SPOON | CHOPPING BOARD | CHOPPING KNIFE | FINE GRATER | TABLESPOON | TEASPOON | PAN FOR ROASTING NUTS

45 ml (3 Tbsp) extra virgin olive oil, plus extra

800 g boneless chicken thighs or drumsticks

salt and pepper, to taste

1 large onion, chopped

3–4 cloves garlic, finely grated or chopped

a few sprigs fresh thyme, woody stalks discarded, plus extra for garnishing

1 large aubergine, cubed

±180 g (1 cup) pitted green olives

30 ml (2 Tbsp) capers (optional)

680 g tomato passata

10 ml (2 tsp) sugar

a handful fresh basil, for serving

finely grated parmesan, for serving (optional)

Heat the oil in a pot over medium-high heat. Fry the chicken briefly in two batches, browning until lightly golden and seasoning with salt and pepper as you go (don't cook it all the way through yet). Remove from the pan with tongs, then add the onion and fry until translucent and soft. Add the garlic and thyme and fry for 1 minute. Stir in the aubergine, olives, capers (if using), tomato passata and sugar, then return the chicken pieces with their juices to the pot, pressing gently to submerge in the sauce. Bring to a simmer, then turn the heat down to low, cover with a lid and cook for 20–25 minutes until the chicken is cooked and tender. Remove from the heat, adjust the seasoning if necessary, then set aside to rest for at least 10 minutes.

Just before serving, finish with a drizzle of olive oil, top with fresh basil, thyme and a sprinkle of parmesan (if using).

Note

· *This dish can just as easily be prepared in a potjie on the open fire.*

Red meat

Rare beef fillet
with mustard cream, rocket and pomegranate

At the height of summer, we're often not in the mood for a plate of steaming hot food. Yet we still love to gather outside around a braai fire, so whatever comes from the grill needs to be light and fresh, something that can perhaps be enjoyed at room temperature. This simple fillet ticks all the boxes (but will still satisfy the die-hard meat lovers), and can be served as part of a beautiful summery spread with multiple salads and icy drinks.

SERVES 4–5

TOOLS: CUTTING BOARD | CHEF'S KNIFE | HOT COALS WITH GRID | BRAAI TONGS | RESTING PLATE FOR MEAT | FOIL (OPTIONAL) | SMALL MIXING BOWL | SPOON | SERVING PLATTER

1 whole beef fillet (800 g–1 kg), trimmed of all visible sinew
±45 ml (3 Tbsp) extra virgin olive oil
salt and pepper, to taste
250 ml (1 cup) sour cream
15 ml (1 Tbsp) Dijon mustard
15 ml (1 Tbsp) wholegrain mustard
a small bunch wild rocket, rinsed
a few Tbsp pomegranate arils (rubies)

Place the fillet on a clean cutting board and rub all over with olive oil, then season generously with salt and pepper. Grill over hot coals (some flames are also fine) on a solid grid for 25–30 minutes in total (depending on the heat of the coals and the height of the grid), turning every 7–8 minutes until evenly brown on all the sides. Leave to rest for at least 15 minutes before carving (cover loosely with foil, if you want to keep it warm). Slice with a very sharp knife into thin slices, then arrange on a serving platter.

Stir the sour cream and both mustards together, then top the meat with dollops all over (serving the rest of the sauce on the side). Garnish with rocket and pomegranate arils, a sprinkle of salt and a generous grinding of black pepper. Serve warm or at room temperature.

Allow about 200 g fillet per person, and adjust the quantities according to the number of guests. If you do have access to a meat thermometer, look for an inner temperature of 60°C for rare, 65°C for medium-rare or 70°C for medium.

Kettle-braaied deboned pork neck
with honey-mustard sauce

I created this dish in 2022 as a pairing for KWV Roodeberg's Reserve red blend – such a successful combo. On the day of the shoot, it surprised the creative team that you could braai a whole pork neck, and that it was so flavourful and easy to slice. Pork neck is an economical cut and highly underrated. It's a wonderful way to entertain a crowd, as it requires little effort and will serve many. A kettle braai with indirect heat over hot coals yields the best result – beautifully smoky and incredibly delicious. But you can also prepare it in a conventional oven. Serve with sides such as The full Monty potato salad (page 81), Roasted butternut (page 105) or Cranberry tabbouleh (page 82).

SERVES 6+

TOOLS: PLATE OR PLATTER | COTTON STRING (OPTIONAL) | PASTRY BRUSH | CHOPPING BOARD | CHOPPING KNIFE | SPOON | KETTLE BRAAI WITH GRID | BRAAI TONGS | MEAT THERMOMETER (OPTIONAL) | BRAAI CASSEROLE (FOR RESTING THE MEAT) | SMALL MIXING BOWL

1.5–2 kg whole deboned pork neck, tied with string (if necessary) to form a log
salt and pepper, to taste
15 ml (1 Tbsp) smoked paprika
30–45 ml (2–3 Tbsp) Dijon mustard
30 ml (2 Tbsp) chopped fresh rosemary

HONEY-MUSTARD SAUCE
45 ml (3 Tbsp) wholegrain mustard
45 ml (3 Tbsp) Dijon mustard
45 ml (3 Tbsp) honey
80 ml (⅓ cup) good quality mayonnaise

FOR KETTLE BRAAI COOKING/ROASTING: Prepare your kettle braai for indirect heat using a full chimney (50–60 briquettes). While you're waiting for the coals to ash over (15–18 minutes), prepare the meat for the fire. Place the pork on a clean plate or platter and season generously on all sides with salt, pepper and smoked paprika. Use a pastry brush to cover the surface all over with mustard or rub it all over with clean hands, then sprinkle the entire surface with the rosemary. Place the pork on a grid directly over the prepared hot coals for a quick grill on both sides (about 2 minutes a side), then transfer the pork to the indirect heat position and cover the kettle braai with a lid, vents open. Roast for 1 hour, then test the inner temperature with a thermometer – it's ready when it reaches 75–80°C. Remove from the heat and leave the meat to rest, covered, for at least 10–15 minutes before carving. Serve thinly carved with the honey-mustard sauce on the side and your choice of salads or sides.

FOR OVEN ROASTING: Place the prepared pork neck on a roasting rack over a roasting dish and roast at 180°C for 60–80 minutes – removing from the heat and checking for inner temperature as described above. Serve as suggested above.

For the sauce, stir all the ingredients together in a mixing bowl. Serve at room temperature, on the side.

Grilled butterflied leg of lamb
with anchovy, garlic and rosemary

I developed this recipe for SA Lamb & Mutton as part of their Heritage Month 2022 campaign, paired with Blaauwklippen's Malbec. It's phenomenal cooked in a smoky kettle braai, but is also suitable for the braai over medium-hot coals (open fire) or roasted in a conventional oven. Don't be afraid of the anchovies – they provide the most delicious savoury flavour that isn't fishy at all. Serve with sides such as toasted pitas, some Tahini yoghurt dip (page 28) or store-bought hummus, Balsamic tomatoes (page 54), and a crisp green salad.

SERVES 6

TOOLS: MORTAR AND PESTLE (SEE NOTE) | CHOPPING BOARD | CHOPPING KNIFE | NON-REACTIVE STAINLESS STEEL OR CERAMIC DISH | MEAT THERMOMETER | DEEP DISH OR BRAAI CASSEROLE | TONGS | ROASTING DISH (FOR CONVENTIONAL OVEN)

6 anchovy fillets (preserved in oil), chopped
4 cloves garlic, finely chopped
finely grated rind and juice of 1 large lemon
45–60 ml (3–4 Tbsp) extra virgin olive oil
1–2 sprigs fresh rosemary, stalks discarded and leaves finely chopped
salt and pepper, to taste
1.5 kg boneless leg of lamb, butterflied

FOR KETTLE BRAAI COOKING/ROASTING: Using a mortar and pestle, grind the anchovies, garlic, lemon rind and juice, olive oil, rosemary and generous amount of seasoning to a runny paste. Place the butterflied leg in a non-reactive dish and rub the paste generously all over the meat. Cover the dish with a lid or with clingfilm, and leave to marinate for at least an hour in a cool place, or for a few hours (even overnight) in the fridge – just return to room temperature before grilling. Prepare your kettle braai for grilling using a full chimney of briquettes (direct and indirect heat), then grill the leg over direct heat on both sides for 2–3 minutes a side, until charred and brown. Move the meat to indirect heat cooking, then cover with the lid, keeping the vents open. Cook for 60–70 minutes until an inserted meat thermometer reaches 65°C (medium-rare). Remove from the heat and leave the meat to rest in a deep dish, covered with a lid or foil, for 10–15 minutes before carving. Serve warm, thinly carved and garnished with extra rosemary if you like, with freshly toasted pita bread, salad, hummus or tahini, etc.

FOR OPEN FIRE GRILLING: Grill on a grid over medium-hot coals, turning with tongs every 8–10 minutes, for about 1 hour in total (the coals will cool with time, so you'll get colour at the beginning and low heat towards the end. Remove from the heat, leave the meat to rest, then serve as above.

FOR OVEN ROASTING: Preheat the oven to 220°C and place the meat fat-side up (butterflied-side down) on a rack positioned over a roasting tray (line the tray with foil, if you like). Roast for 20 minutes then turn down the heat to 160°C and continue to roast for another 40–50 minutes. Remove from the oven, leave the meat to rest, then serve as above.

Note

• If you don't have a pestle and mortar, chop the marinade ingredients together (without liquids) as finely as possible, then mix with the oil, lemon juice, salt and pepper.

Asian-style BBQ pork loin ribs

I don't prepare ribs often, but when I do, this recipe is lip-smackingly delicious. As with many other sweet marinades, it is best to par-cook the meat in the marinade until it almost falls from the bone, then finish it over medium-hot coals until sticky and glossy. Hoisin sauce is the hero here – available in the Asian food section of many good supermarkets.

SERVES 4

TOOLS: WOODEN SPOON | LARGE POT WITH LID | COARSE GRATER | FINE GRATER | FIRE WITH MEDIUM-HOT COALS | HINGED GRID OR OPEN GRID | WORKING SURFACE | CUTTING BOARD | SHARP KNIFE | BOX GRATER | FINE GRATER | BASTING BRUSH | BRAAI TONGS | STIRRING SPOON

30 ml (2 Tbsp) vegetable oil
1 onion, roughly grated
4 cloves garlic, finely grated
30 ml (2 Tbsp) finely grated fresh ginger
125 ml (½ cup) hoisin sauce
60 ml (¼ cup) honey
45 ml (3 Tbsp) soy sauce
30 ml (2 Tbsp) white vinegar
15 ml (1 Tbsp) sesame oil
4 large pork loin rib racks (fresh, not smoked)
a small bunch spring onions, sliced, for serving

To a large pot, add the vegetable oil, onion, garlic, ginger, hoisin sauce, honey, soy sauce, vinegar and sesame oil. Stir, then add the rib racks (cut them in half to fit into the pot, if necessary). Cover the pot with a lid and bring to a simmer over a low heat for at least 1 hour or until the meat is very tender and almost falling off the bone (turn the ribs halfway to coat all sides in the sauce), stirring the bottom from time to time to prevent burning. Remove the ribs from the pot and bring the sauce to a rolling boil, reducing it by about a third until it reaches the consistency of a runny chutney. Grill the ribs over medium-hot coals on both sides, basting with the reduced marinade, until glossy and sticky and slightly charred, then remove from the heat. Serve hot, scattered with spring onions.

Cape mutton tomato bredie

In 2020 I created this recipe for Anthonij Rupert Wines' Cape of Good Hope Syrah. The gentle, perfumed fragrance of this popular Cape heritage stew will seduce you into second helpings – it's not a curry, so don't expect 'hot and spicy.' The magic lies in using just a few key spices and a generous amount of fresh, ripe tomatoes; canned tomatoes simply won't give the same result. Prepare the bredie in a large pot on a (gas) hob/cooker or in a potjie over the fire.

SERVES 6

TOOLS: CHOPPING BOARD | CHOPPING KNIFE | FINE GRATER | 2 BOWLS (FOR CHOPPED TOMATOES AND HALVED POTATOES) | LARGE HEAVY-BASED POT (WITH A LID) WITH HEAT SOURCE OR LARGE CAST-IRON POTJIE WITH FIRE AND POTJIE STAND | PLATE FOR SEARED MEAT | WOODEN SPOON | MEDIUM POT FOR COOKING RICE

45 ml (3 Tbsp) olive oil or vegetable oil

1.5 kg mutton rib chunks or neck chops or stewing chunks

salt and pepper, to taste

2 onions, chopped

10 whole peppercorns or 5 ml (1 tsp) ground white pepper

5 ml (1 tsp) whole cloves

6 whole cardamom pods

2 cinnamon sticks

2 cloves garlic, finely grated

30 ml (2 Tbsp) finely grated fresh ginger

1–1.2 kg ripe tomatoes, diced

5–10 ml (1–2 tsp) sugar

750 g baby potatoes, rinsed and halved

cooked jasmine or basmati rice, for serving

a handful fresh coriander, roughly chopped, for serving (optional)

Heat the oil in a large pot over medium-high heat. Add the meat and fry (in batches) on the fatty sides until light brown, seasoning with salt and pepper as you go. Remove the meat from the pot and turn down the heat to low. Add the onions, peppercorns, whole cloves, cardamom and cinnamon sticks. Fry until the onions are translucent and soft, stirring often (take your time). Add the garlic and ginger and fry for another minute. Add the tomatoes and sugar, and stir to loosen any sticky bits at the bottom of the pot. Bring the mixture to a simmer, then return the meat to the pot and stir (the tomatoes will break down into a sauce over time). Cover with a lid and simmer over low heat for about 1½ hours. Add the potatoes and stir to cover them in liquid, then cover and simmer for another 30 minutes or until the potatoes are tender and the meat is starting to fall off the bone. Taste and adjust the seasoning if necessary. Serve warm with fluffy rice and a scattering of fresh coriander (if using).

Keep the diced potatoes covered in water before adding them to the pot, to prevent discolouration. If you can find them, remove the cardamom pods and cinnamon sticks at the end of the cooking process.

Red wine-braised venison stew

As a child I ate a lot of venison pie; my mother made it often because my father loved to hunt. Although venison pie is delectable, it's also a labour of love. So these days I mostly skip the pastry part, add some French bourguignon inspiration and serve it over rice or a creamy polenta. It serves a crowd and can be made on the stove top or in a large potjie over a fire.

SERVES 6–8

TOOLS: LARGE BOWL | VERY LARGE CAST-IRON POT OR POTJIE WITH HEAT SOURCE | WOODEN SPOON | CHOPPING BOARD | CHOPPING KNIFE | PEELER | PESTLE AND MORTAR

80 ml (⅓ cup) cake wheat flour

1.5 kg boneless venison, cut into chunks (I used gemsbok)

45 ml (3 Tbsp) olive oil

salt and pepper, to taste

250 g streaky bacon, chopped

2 carrots, peeled and finely chopped

1 onion, finely chopped

750 ml (3 cups) baby onions, peeled

10 ml (2 tsp) ground coriander

5 ml (1 tsp) ground white pepper

5 ml (1 tsp) juniper berries, ground in a pestle and mortar

2 bay leaves

30 ml (2 Tbsp) tomato paste

375 ml (1½ cups) dry red wine

375 ml (1½ cups) beef stock

30 ml (2 Tbsp) balsamic vinegar

250 g portabellini mushrooms, halved

30 ml (2 Tbsp) smooth apricot jam (optional)

a handful fresh Italian parsley, finely chopped, for serving

Add the flour to a large bowl, then toss the meat chunks to coat all over. Heat the oil in a large cast-iron pot or potjie, then fry the floured chunks over high heat in batches until slightly browned, but not fully cooked. Season with salt and pepper, then remove from the pot and set aside. Turn down the heat to medium, add the bacon, carrots, chopped onion and whole baby onions to the pot, then fry until the bacon turns lightly brown, scraping the bottom (add a splash of water if the bottom is too sticky). Add the coriander, pepper, juniper berries, bay leaves and tomato paste, stirring for a minute, then pour in the wine, stock and vinegar. Stir and bring to a simmer, then return the meat to the pot and press gently to submerge. Cook, covered, for about 1½ hours or until very tender.

Add the mushrooms and jam (if using), stirring, and simmer for another 15 minutes until cooked. Taste and add more salt and pepper if needed. Serve warm, scattered with parsley, with rice or creamy polenta or with crusty bread for dipping.

You can substitute the venison with beef or mutton.

Sweet
endings

Marinated spiced fruit salad

My darling Aunt Wilma Smit – a master embroiderer from Oudtshoorn – and her husband Johan recently celebrated their 50th wedding anniversary with a scrumptious lunch for extended family and friends. As part of the dessert buffet, they served legendary French chef Alain Senderens's recipe for a chilled fruit salad in a light syrup infused with cloves, vanilla, ginger, citrus, etc. It reminded me again how simplicity can be cleverly elevated. This is my version of the original recipe; use whatever seasonal fruit you have on hand and marinate it in the syrup for no longer than 3 hours to maintain the cut fruit's natural freshness.

SERVES 6

TOOLS: MEDIUM POT OR SAUCEPAN | WOODEN SPOON | CUP MEASURE | PEELER | CHOPPING BOARD | CHOPPING KNIFE | PARING KNIFE | SALAD BOWL

100 g (½ cup) white sugar
500 ml (2 cups) water
1 vanilla pod, sliced lengthways and seeds scraped out
2 whole cloves
1 whole star anise
1 cinnamon stick
peeled zest 1 lime
peeled zest ½ lemon
a few slices fresh ginger
a few fresh mint leaves, plus extra, for serving
±8 cups sliced fruit of your choice (e.g. papaya, mango, watermelon, strawberries, nectarines, peaches, kiwi, litchi, grapes)

In a pot or saucepan over medium heat, add the sugar, water, scraped vanilla seeds and pod, whole cloves, star anise, cinnamon, lime and lemon zest, ginger and mint leaves. Bring to a simmer, stirring, then remove from the heat as soon as the sugar has dissolved. Leave to infuse until completely cool (this may be done a day or two ahead), then strain through a sieve, discarding the solids. Arrange the sliced fruit in a bowl, pour over the syrup, stir gently, and leave to marinate in the fridge for 2–3 hours before serving. Stir again before serving, then top with a few mint leaves and serve cold, with or without vanilla ice cream.

Tropical Eton mess

When dining outdoors casually, no-one wants to make a fussy, time-consuming dessert. Store-bought meringues, fresh fruit and cream are always a good idea – it's light, simple and mostly gluten free. When passion fruit isn't in season, the canned pulp can be readily found all year round in most supermarkets and provides a delicious saucy base. Change up the fresh fruit according to the season and what you love, set up a self-help station and let everyone assemble their own.

SERVES 4–6

TOOLS: CHOPPING BOARD | CHOPPING KNIFE | PARING KNIFE | NON-REACTIVE GLASS OR CERAMIC MIXING BOWL | FINE GRATER | TABLESPOON | BALLOON WHISK (OR ELECTRIC HAND WHISK) | SERVING BOWLS OR GLASSES AND SPOONS

1–2 ripe mangoes, peeled and sliced
3–4 ripe kiwi fruit, peeled and sliced
12–15 Cape gooseberries
16–24 mini vanilla meringues (store-bought)
±230 g (¾ cup) passion fruit pulp, fresh or canned
250 ml (1 cup) fresh cream, chilled
a few fresh limes (optional)

PREPARE A SELF-HELP DESSERT STATION: Place serving bowls or glasses with spoons on a table, put the meringues in a serving bowl and the fruit in separate bowls, with serving spoons. When you're ready to serve, use a manual balloon whisk (or electric hand whisk) to softly whip the cream in a mixing bowl to soft peaks (it only takes a few minutes), then place it alongside the fruit and meringues, along with a few limes and a fine grater. To assemble, guests can spoon layers of (crushed, if they like) meringue, sliced fruit, whipped cream and passion fruit pulp into their bowls, topping it with freshly grated lime rind (if using).

Notes

- *The addition of lime zest provides a lovely sharp edge to almost any fruit.*

- *If you don't like whipped cream, substitute it with double cream plain yoghurt for a slightly tarter result, or make a mixture of the two by folding them together in a bowl.*

- *If you prefer sweetened cream, add 10 ml (2 tsp) castor sugar as well as a dash of vanilla extract to your fresh cream before whisking.*

- *If you love sweet cream but would prefer not to have to whisk it, substitute the fresh cream for a cheeky can of sweetened whipped cream with a convenient spout (super popular with kids!).*

Easy chocolate sauce *for ice cream*

I grew up in a home in which my mother adored vanilla ice cream and chocolate sauce. She loved it so much that we had it for dessert a few times a week – she bought 5-litre tubs of affordable ice cream and made her chocolate sauce from a few pantry staples - a thin but full-flavoured warm sauce that melts your ice cream into creamy pools. I've since tweaked my mom's original recipe a little, as I prefer a slightly darker, thicker sauce with a little less sugar. The key to a full-flavoured chocolate sauce is to make it with water or a little milk (not cream) and to add a generous pinch of salt. This sauce may be made ahead and is easily reheated. It will last for 3–5 days in the fridge, covered.

MAKES ±375 ML (1½ CUPS)

TOOLS: SMALL POT OR SAUCEPAN | CUP MEASURE | TABLESPOON | WOODEN SPOON | TEASPOON

125 ml (½ cup) sugar

60 ml (¼ cup) cocoa powder

125 ml (½ cup) hot water

125 ml (½ cup) milk

30 ml (2 Tbsp) butter

5 ml (1 tsp) vanilla extract

a pinch salt

50 g dark chocolate, broken into blocks (optional)

Mix the sugar and cocoa powder together in a pot or saucepan. Add the hot water, stir well, then add the milk and butter. Place over medium heat, stirring until the sugar melts and the mixture comes to a simmer. Remove the pot from the heat, then stir in the vanilla and salt. For a luxurious twist, add the dark chocolate (if using) to the warm sauce and stir every few minutes until fully melted and smooth. Serve warm over vanilla ice cream, ideally topped with roughly chopped pecan nuts or peanuts.

Honey caramel almond sauce *for ice cream*

One of my Keurbooms friends, André van Niekerk, recently shared his late mother Theresa van Niekerk's recipe for this sauce with me. She was an excellent cook and regularly entertained esteemed guests from all over the world, serving this sauce with vanilla ice cream, always to everyone's delight. I adore almonds, and I love the combination of the honey and brown sugar – it delivers an elegantly balanced sauce that is so much more than mere caramel. I've added a generous pinch of salt, but it's an optional extra.

MAKES ±325 ML/SERVES 4

TOOLS: SAUCEPAN | WOODEN SPOON | PAN FOR ROASTING ALMONDS

60 ml (¼ cup) soft brown sugar

60 ml (¼ cup) honey

125 ml (½ cup) fresh cream

60 g (¼ cup) butter

5 ml (1 tsp) vanilla extract

a pinch salt (optional)

125 ml (½ cup) flaked almonds, lightly roasted

Place the sugar, honey, cream and butter in a small saucepan and stir over medium heat, until the sugar and the butter have melted. Bring to a simmer, turn down the heat to low, and cook for 5–10 minutes (be careful not to let it boil over; stir often). Remove from the heat, add the vanilla, salt (if using) and half the almonds, then stir. Serve warm over vanilla ice cream, topped with the remaining roasted almonds.

Caramel 'cheesecakettes'

I recently wanted to devise a recipe that resembled a no-bake cheesecake, with a filling based on a peppermint crisp tart, yet easy enough so that there would be no heavy whisking involved – something fun that could be assembled and enjoyed immediately after mixing. This is the result – a totally delicious caramel cheesecake mixture made with cottage cheese, canned caramel and fresh cream – spread over digestive cookies and topped with raspberries. The cookies are delightfully crisp if eaten immediately, but they soften to a pliant, 'forkable' texture after a few hours of refrigeration, thus easy to make ahead.

SERVES 6

TOOLS: FORK | MIXING BOWL | BALLOON WHISK | SPOON | CHOPPING KNIFE | 6 SERVING GLASSES (COOLDRINK, WHISKY, WINE, WITH A CAPACITY OF ±180 ML)

1 × 250 g tub smooth full cream plain cottage cheese (see Note)
60–125 ml (¼–½ cup) fresh cream
1 × 360 g can Nestlé Caramel Treat
a pinch salt
200 g digestive biscuits
250 g fresh raspberries
salt flakes, for garnishing (optional)

Mash the cottage cheese and half the cream together in a bowl, first with a fork and then mixing with a balloon whisk until smooth – it should be a luxuriously thick, super-smooth mixture that can hold its shape, so don't add all the cream if you don't need to. Stir the caramel in the can to loosen it, then add it to the cottage cheese mixture along with the pinch of salt, stirring with the whisk until it's smooth and free of any lumps. Spoon some of the mixture onto each biscuit, then top with raspberries and salt flakes (if using). Serve at once, or cover (in a deep, flat container with a lid) and refrigerate until ready to serve.

Notes

- Not all brands of full cream smooth cottage cheese react the same – some need less cream to become luxuriously smooth and blended, so start with a few tablespoons of cream and continue to add more as required.

- The mixture will continue to set and become more stable once refrigerated, but the cookies will become less crispy. Choose which option you prefer – soft cream with crisp biscuits, or thicker cream with soft biscuits.

The mixture, crushed biscuits and berries may also be assembled in layers in small dessert glasses, served with spoons.

Recipe index

Thank you

I am eternally grateful to be co-creating with the best team anyone could wish for. Firstly, Tasha Seccombe, you turn my humble cooking into art! Thank you for all the hours of driving, for all the fabulous pastries and treats, for always bringing more than your A-game, for relentlessly pursuing excellence and for being the best friend I could ask for, through the sweat and tears, but also the victories and laughter. You inspire me with your boundless talents, your wisdom and your human insight. May we continue to create many more books together.

To the dream team at Penguin Random House – Beverley Dodd, Aimee Carelse, Helen Henn, Cecilia Barfield and Joy Nel – thank you for giving me another opportunity to do what I love most. What a pleasure and privilege it is to be guided and supported by such a stellar publishing squad.

Thank you Chantal Kondlo for patiently washing all the dishes and cleaning up at the photoshoots – it was such a pleasure to have your positive spirit in my kitchen, always smiling.

A big thank you to Comine Claassen from Jangroentjie Cottage on Klipheuvel Farm for providing us with the location for the lifestyle images. Your generosity knows no bounds. We couldn't have asked for a more beautiful setting to capture the essence of al fresco. Thank you also to my family and friends who generously gave their time to be in our lifestyle shoot – Erna and Gerhard Compion, Marni and Christo Bezuidenhout, Maaika Kruger and Chantal Kondlo. Thank you Gerhard for the fabulous fish for the third time around – I'm so lucky to have a trout farmer brother-in-law on speed dial.

To Schalk and Valki, who have always been my biggest supporters and who patiently tolerate the kitchen and studio chaos, year after year: thank you from the bottom of my heart.

Ilse x

Published in 2023 by Penguin Books
an imprint of Penguin Random House
South Africa (Pty) Ltd
Company Reg. No. 1953/000441/07
The Estuaries, 4 Oxbow Crescent, Century Avenue,
Century City 7441, Cape Town, South Africa
PO Box 1144, Cape Town, 8000, South Africa

Reprinted in 2024

www.penguinrandomhouse.co.za

Publisher: Beverley Dodd
Managing editor: Aimee Sinclair
Designer: Helen Henn
Editor and indexer: Cecilia Barfield
Proofreader: Joy Nel
Photographer: Tasha Seccombe
Food and prop stylists: Ilse van der Merwe
    and Tasha Seccombe
Food preparation: Ilse van der Merwe

Reproduction: Studio Repro, Cape Town
Printed and bound in China by 1010 Printing
International Ltd.

ISBN: 978-1-48590-159-4